*Newmarket — Me*

*For Elisabeth*

# NEWMARKET
# MEDIEVAL AND TUDOR

## by Peter May

with an Appendix on
The Archaeology of Newmarket
by Ivan E. Moore

Foreword by
David Dymond

Published privately
1982

© Peter May, 1982

ISBN 0 9503024 5 7

Designed, typeset in IBM Press Roman and produced by
Margaret Helps & Associates, King's Lynn, Norfolk

Printed in England by
The Witley Press, Hunstanton, Norfolk

# Contents

## Donors and Subscribers

The author is most grateful to the following whose generous donations and subscriptions have made possible the publication of this book:

Barclays Bank Limited
Bennett's Bookshop
G. Buck
E. and C. Cooper
H. Day
Dr J. H. Dean
Dr A. Dossetor
Ennions
R. and S. Evans
T. J. Fallon
Forest Heath District Council
S. Gibson
Colonel D. Gray
Greene King & Sons Limited
R. J. Hannam
J. Hindley
B. Hobbs
Colonel R. Hutchison
Jackson-Stops and Staff
The Jockey Club
K. Kemp-Turner
Lloyds Bank Limited

Mrs G. McCalmont
N. Mayes Limited
R. Merryweather
Moulton & District Newsround
Newmarket Upper School
Dr T. Pollock
G. Pritchard-Gordon
Pye Electro-Devices Limited
J. Richardson
Rotary Club of Newmarket
Simpson & Jeffery
W. B. Singleton
M. Skelton
F. S. Snow
M. Stoute
R. D. Tanner
Tattersalls Limited
Miss M. Taylor
Tindall & Son
Mrs D. Webb
Mrs Woollard
F. W. Woolworth & Co. Ltd

## List of Illustrations

For those who have forgotten or have never been familiar with the old coinage, the pound (£ = latin *libra*) was made up of 20 shillings, abbreviated s (from the latin *solidi*), or of 240 pennies, abbreviated d (from the latin *denarii*). The shilling was made up of 12 pennies; the penny itself could be broken up into half-pennies (½d) or farthings (¼d and ¾d).

Amounts such as 26s 8d, 13s 4d, 6s 8d, 3s 4d and 20d, which frequently occur in medieval documents, may puzzle modern readers. A normal unit of accounting was the mark (13s 4d), not itself a coin, and these amounts are multiples or fractions of the mark, for example 6s 8d was half a mark and 26s 8d was two marks.

As to the present value of the sums of money mentioned, a multiple of forty has been suggested by one scholar for the years 1450 and 1950. No comparison is, however, really possible since we live today in a completely different world where inflation among other things makes nonsense of any such multiplication.

## Foreword

I heartily recommend this book to local people curious about their surroundings and to all those interested in the development of towns. Architecturally Newmarket may not be one of the most attractive places in Suffolk, but it undoubtedly has a fascinating and unusual history. Canon Peter May, who until 1978 was Rector of St Mary's Church, has now distilled years of research into a book which will immediately rank among the best town histories of East Anglia. Whereas medieval local history is usually presented as a few miscellaneous facts and guesses, if dealt with at all, we here gain a genuine insight into the workings of a small medieval town, administratively, economically and socially.

Many of us think of Newmarket as an international centre of horse breeding, training and racing, and as the traditional haunt of royalty and nobility. Of course those aspects have been of great importance since 1600, but this book is concerned with the town's early or 'fundamental' history. At around 1200 the Argentein family established a speculative 'new market', in order to exploit the prehistoric high-road into, and out of, East Anglia. Long before horse racing became significant, its market, fairs, shops and inns served local residents, the surrounding rural area, and travellers of all kinds. Furthermore, being a relatively late and artificial creation, Newmarket has always had the air of a 'frontier town', never quite sure of its allegiance to east or west. It is no accident, as Peter May shows, that from its earliest days the town lay in two manors, two parishes and two counties.

Finally, on behalf of his many friends, I would like to wish Peter May a full recovery from his recent illness. We look forward to reading his second volume on the new, 'royal' Newmarket.

*David Dymond*

## Preface and Acknowledgements

The history of Newmarket may be divided into two parts, first from its beginnings in the 13th century to 1600, second from King James I's choice of Newmarket for his palace at the beginning of the 17th century up to the present day. Previous historians have more or less ignored the first part of Newmarket's history and have concentrated somewhat naturally on its more interesting history from 1600; in so doing they seem to have tacitly assumed that Newmarket from its very beginning was in embryo the horse racing and stud world it is predominantly today. It appears to me fairly conclusive that no one living in 1600 could possibly have imagined that within twenty-five years Newmarket would have become the site of a royal palace and in the 20th century the centre of horse racing and breeding in England, if not in the world. Of course its history has been continuous from its beginnings to the present day, but the change in its fortunes at the beginning of the 17th century was so great that it seemed simplest to divide its history there. This volume therefore is concerned with its birth in the 13th century to the end of the 16th century. I hope in due course to write a second volume to bring the story up to date.

Throughout the reading of this book constant reference should be made to the plan of Newmarket as it may have been in 1472, to be found on pages 32 and 33.

Newmarket was in this first stage of its history too insignificant a place to attract its own illustrators. I have had therefore to find from contemporary sources the kind of illustrations which appear to me to illuminate important aspects of its life. I am grateful to the following for permission to use photographs supplied by them: the British Library for illustrations 8 and 14, Cambridge University Library for illustrations 1, 2, 5, 9, 10, 11, 13, 15, 17 and 18, the Suffolk Record Office at Ipswich for illustrations 3, 7, 12 and 16 and for plan C, and to the Cambridgeshire Collection, Cambridgeshire Libraries for illustration 6.

Four of the plans were drawn for me by my nephew Michael Winterbottom, to whom my thanks are due for so professional a job. I am grateful to Nigel Bloxham for his photograph of the Gough Map (A) and to Forest Heath District Council for the plan of Newmarket as it is today (H).

This book would not have been written without the encouragement of the present lord of the manor of Newmarket, Dr Idries Shah, who invited me to write it and has permitted me to make extensive use of the court rolls of his manor in the Suffolk Record Office at Bury St Edmunds. I am particularly grateful to Professor Ornstein, President of the Institute for the Study of Human Knowledge, California, for making a very generous grant, on Dr Shah's recommendation, towards the publication of this book.

It would not be possible to estimate how much I owe to David Dymond and Peter Northeast who at every stage have encouraged me with their criticism and comments, and have generously allowed me to dip into their store of local history in general and of Newmarket in particular. I am grateful especially to David Dymond not only for writing the foreword but also, with his wife, for reading the proofs and seeing the manuscript through the press. Ivan Moore was good enough to contribute an appendix on the archaeology of Newmarket.

Most of the responsibility for publishing this book has fallen on the shoulders of Margaret Helps of King's Lynn; her interest in local history and her technical skills as sales-promoter and typesetter have been major factors in its attractive presentation. I am deeply grateful to her, and also to Basil Browes who has acted as treasurer for the whole project.

Finally I can only hope that this book will give as much enjoyment to its readers as it has to its author.

*April 1982* *Peter May*

## Chapter One

# THE BEGINNINGS

Most Suffolk towns and villages are recorded specifically by name in Domesday Book and therefore have their beginnings in history well before 1086 when Domesday Book was compiled. Unfortunately the scarcity of documentary sources before 1086 means that their beginnings are generally obscure and difficult to determine. For example, the name Exning (or *Esselinga* as it is in Domesday Book) means the people of Gixa, and has nothing to do with the Iceni or Boudicca; beyond the fact that at some period in history the people of Gixa settled round what we now know as Exning and gave their name to it, its beginnings are difficult to determine. Not so with Newmarket. It is not recorded specifically by name in Domesday Book; no doubt the area later occupied by Newmarket is included in the entries for Exning (*Esselinga*) and Woodditton (*Ditone*). Because it is a relatively new town, documentary sources enable us to pinpoint within fifty years when it came into being, and to give us some indications how it came into being.

If we look at a map of the district and trace the boundaries of the various parishes on either side of the A 11, from Six Mile Bottom to Newmarket, and then of the A 45 on to Kentford, we discover that these roads roughly mark the boundary lines between the parishes. On the north side we have Bottisham, the Swaffhams, Burwell, Exning, Snailwell and Chippenham; the centres of these villages are, for the most part, on the edge of the Fens, with lodes running down to the Cam on the one side, and with pasture lands stretching out on the other side over the chalkland to the A 11. On the south side we have Brinkley, Westley Waterless, Dullingham, Stetchworth, Woodditton, Cheveley, Ashley and Moulton; the centres of these villages are on the western side of the boulder clay, with their former pasture lands reaching north-west to the A 11 and the A 45. Exning and Snailwell are somewhat different from all these villages in that they are much more typically agricultural.

These parish boundaries are very ancient, going back beyond Domesday; the A 11 and the A 45 were not of course then the kind of road that they are today; they correspond roughly to the old Icknield Way, which was then not so much a road as a series of trackways running all the way from Norfolk to Wessex. Clearly for all these parishes the Icknield Way was a convenient parish boundary along the chalk ridge. The only two parishes which straddle the Icknield Way are Kentford and Newmarket; Kentford does so because the Icknield Way there crossed the river Kennet, and it was natural for a village to grow up round a river crossing. Newmarket is much later than any of these other villages; and we may ask therefore why it too straddles the Icknield Way.

The fact is that Newmarket only does so because it was carved out of one parish (Exning) and spread out into another (Woodditton). The boundaries of these two parishes met, like the other villages we have mentioned, on the Icknield Way; until it became an administrative unit in its own right early in the 16th century, the northern part of Newmarket, corresponding to the old St Mary's Ward, was in Exning, in Suffolk, while the southern part, corresponding to the old All Saints' Ward, was in Woodditton, in Cambridgeshire. Newmarket thus straddled not only the Icknield Way but also the county boundary between Suffolk and Cambridgeshire; this complicates matters for the local historian because he has not one but two county records to consult.

We first begin to find references to Newmarket about 1220. In 1219 one Walkelin was in contention with Geoffrey and his wife Phyllis of Snailwell about an acre and a half of land in Newmarket (the latin is *novum mercatum*).[1] In 1220 an enquiry found that there were nineteen ploughteams at work in the 'vill' of Ixnyng and New Market.[2] Finally in 1223 (confirmed in 1227) King Henry III gave Richard Argentein the right to hold a fair at his manor of New Market for three days every year around St Giles' Day (1 September).[3] Clearly a new market had been created before 1219 and established by 1223. A hundred or so years later a new market was literally on the map, on Gough's map of Great Britain now in the Bodleian Library at Oxford, dated 1325–1350; it shows neither of its parent parishes, Exning and Woodditton (see map A on page 3). There were incidentally many other places, especially in the south-west of England, which acquired new markets at about this time, and could easily have been named Newmarket; in fact the atlas directory gives only two other places so named in the British Isles, one on the Isle of Lewis, and the other, Hesket Newmarket, in Cumbria.

Nonetheless, although our Newmarket was in existence by 1220 and was literally on the map by 1350, it was not recognised as a separate unit either administratively or ecclesiastically until much later. Administratively it was included for taxation purposes in Exning or Woodditton. Thus in the Hundred Rolls for Cambridgeshire of 1279, in the Hundred of Cheveley the Prior of Fordham had five tenants in Newmarket (not otherwise mentioned);[4] in the same rolls for the half Hundred of Exning in Suffolk Newmarket is not mentioned.[5] In the Cambridgeshire Subsidy Rolls of 1327 Newmarket is included under Woodditton (with its manors of Ditton Camoys, Ditton Valens, Saxton with Newmarket and Wick);[6] in the Suffolk Subsidy Rolls of the same date there is no mention of Newmarket under the township of Exning, although we know from other sources that residents of Newmarket are included in the Exning list.[7] In the *Inquisitiones Nonarum* of 1341 it is presumably included in Cambridgeshire under Woodditton with its different manors;[8] in those for Suffolk Newmarket is not mentioned by name, although again there appear to be some Newmarket residents included in the list.[9] By 1524 however it was certainly accepted as a separate taxation unit, with forty-two persons mentioned by name, and some £7 collected.[10]

Ecclesiastically St Mary's Church, built in the late 13th century, was called the old chapel of the Blessed Mary in Newmarket and was a chapel of ease in the parish of St Martin, Exning, until the beginning of the 16th century when it became a parish church. All Saints' Church in Newmarket, which was built later than St Mary's and seems to have been called the new chapel of the Blessed Mary at one time, was a chapel of ease in the parish of All Saints', Woodditton, until 1868 when it became a parish in its own right.

The inclusion of Newmarket both administratively and ecclesiastically within the parishes of Exning and Woodditton until comparatively late in its history suggests that in its early days it existed, as its name implies, primarily as a market, a new market, appended to and dependent on Exning and Woodditton. How and why did this new market come into existence?

### Newmarket's Origin

The most popular and widely spread explanation of Newmarket's origin is that in 1227 the plague came to Exning, at that time a flourishing market centre, and the market was transferred to a new site at Newmarket. There are two main reasons why this explanation of Newmarket's origin is no longer tenable.

First there is no evidence that Exning had a market and was a flourishing market centre in 1227. It was not until 1257 (nearly forty years *after* the first mention of Newmarket by name) that William de Valens, lord of one of the Exning manors, received a charter from King Henry III to have a market every Monday at his Exning manor.[11] If there had been an earlier market there, we might have expected some reference to it in the charter; indeed we may wonder whether there would have been any need to apply for a charter for a market if there had been one there only thirty years earlier. In fact William de Valens never seems to have taken up his charter. Some thirty years later in 1287 King Edward I was clamping down on the privileges claimed by lords of manors; William de Valens claimed that he had the right to the fines accruing from breaches of the regulations for the making and selling of bread and ale in Exning, but he did not claim, as Reginald Argentein did for Newmarket, that he had been granted the right to hold a market there.[12]

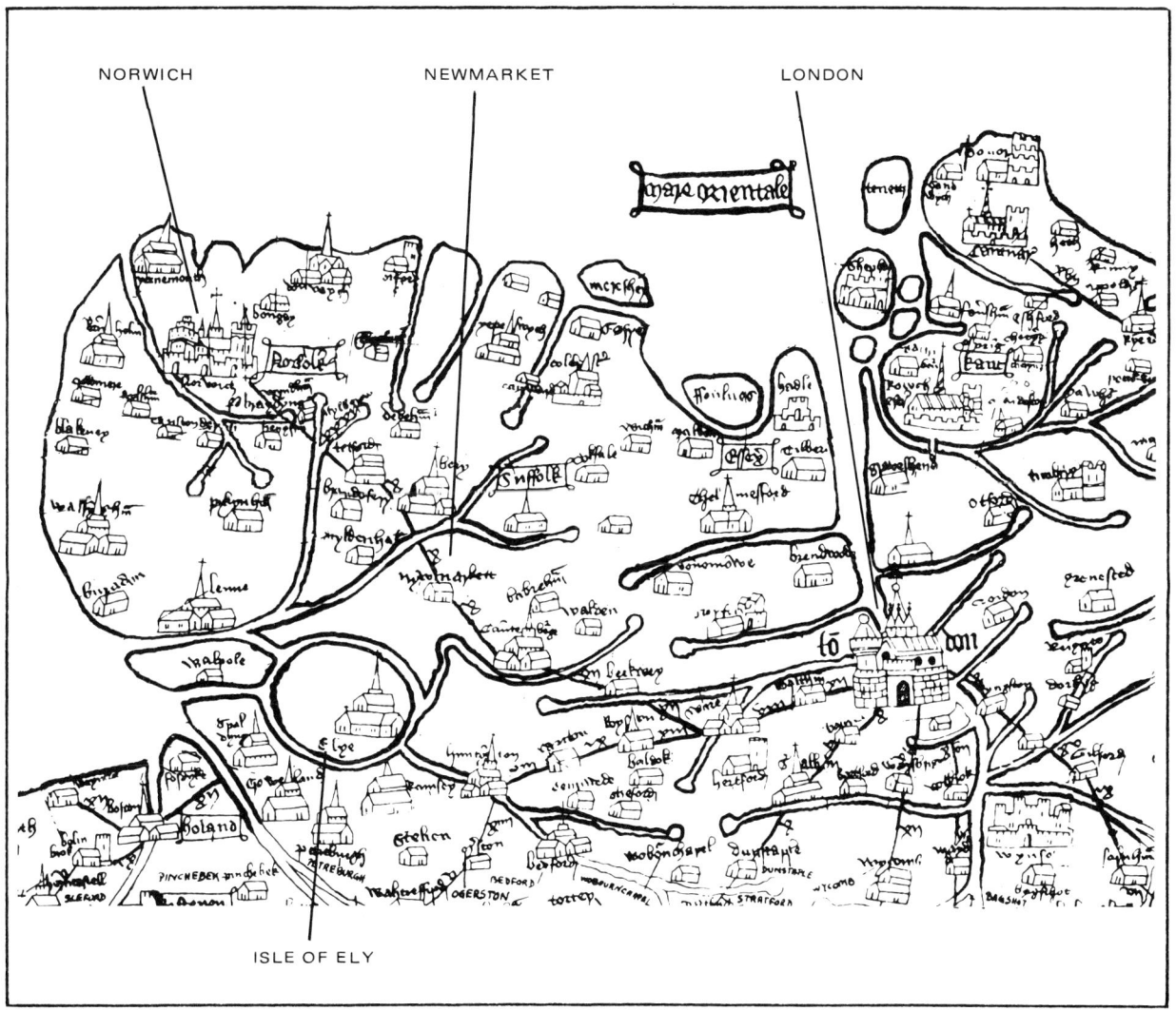

NORWICH        NEWMARKET        LONDON

ISLE OF ELY

**Map A**

A section of Gough's map of Britain, dated 1325–1350, now in the Bodleian Library of Oxford, showing the London to Norwich road, running through Ware, Barkway, Cambridge, Newmarket and Thetford.

It is important to realise that the map was drawn with North to the left.

Note the Isle of Ely and the geographer's assumption that rivers originated in ponds.

It seems very unlikely therefore that Exning had a market before 1220 which could have been transferred to Newmarket. It is however only fair to say that Exning was a flourishing place and may well have had its own market *before* the Norman Conquest of 1066, but its taxable value had been drastically reduced from £56 in the time of King Edward the Confessor to £12 'when received'.[13] It has been suggested that this drastic reduction was due to the destruction of its agricultural assets, as a punishment for being the place in which a revolt against King William I had been initiated by Ralph de Gael and Roger, Earl of Hereford, on the occasion of Ralph's marriage to Roger's daughter at Exning in 1075.[14] It may well have been that part of Exning's punishment was the withdrawal of its market, always a source of profit to the lord of the manor.

The second reason why we no longer accept the plague tradition of Newmarket's origin is that the tradition itself is only 150 years old. The tradition that Newmarket originated as a result of a plague in Exning is first mentioned in a directory of 1830 which states: 'The market is supposed to have been removed from Exning in consequence of contagion, in the year 1227'.[15] It seems likely that the editor's source of information was the then Vicar of Exning, Dr Thomas Dibdin, who published a history of Exning in 1832 in which he puts forward the theory of the plague.[16] At all events none of the several topographers who wrote about Exning and Newmarket *before* 1830 know of the plague origin of Newmarket, and we must therefore discount it as having any historical basis. We can easily understand how such a tradition could arise. A local historian, trying to explain Exning's early importance and its decline in the light of Newmarket's rise, could find an easy explanation in a plague. The isolation of many a church in Suffolk is likewise attributed to the same reason, although in fact the Black Death appears to have been the cause of the isolation of only one church in Suffolk in 1349.[17]

It seems therefore fairly conclusive that Newmarket did not originate as a result of a plague at Exning. How then did it originate? There are two suggested answers. Professor Beresford argues that Newmarket is a planned town, that is, the lord of the manor deliberately laid down a market and built a small township around it.[18] Professor Hoskins says: 'More probably the town grew up *naturally* along a busy medieval road' (my italics).[19] In either case the key figure is the lord of the manor. We have already seen that in 1227 Richard Argentein obtained a charter from King Henry III for a fair at his manor of Newmarket. The first reference to Newmarket's origin appears to be in the first English edition (1610) of Camden's *Britannia*. There we read: 'Under King Henrie the third [1216–1272] Sir Robert L'Isle [de Insula] gave one part of it [Newmarket] in franke marriage with his daughter Cassandra unto Sir Richard de Argentein'.[20] In 1167 Robert de Insula and his wife Galliena had been granted land in Exning called Porter's Manor.[21] No doubt it was part of this land that Robert gave as dowry to Cassandra on her wedding to Richard Argentein. At all events we know that in 1210 Richard had 40 shillings' worth of land in Exning, perhaps 120 acres at 4d an acre.[22]

The question is: did Richard Argentein, as Professor Beresford argues, deliberately establish a market and build up a small town around it, or did the market more or less naturally grow up, as Professor Hoskins suggests? It is indeed possible that there was already a market there before Richard and Cassandra received it on their wedding day; this might perhaps explain why we have no charter recording the grant of a market in Newmarket. The evidence, as we shall see, seems on the whole to support a natural growth rather than a planned one.

The basic fact is that the great London to Norwich road converged with the Icknield Way at the spot which we now know as Newmarket. Moreover Newmarket is halfway between Cambridge and Mildenhall, about ten miles each way, a reasonable day's journey for the average traveller of the time; the Gough map, to which we have already referred, marks 'Naymarkett' as being ten miles from 'Myldenhal' and ten miles from 'Cauntebrige' (see the reproduction of the relevant portion of this map on page 3). Further a map shows that Newmarket is a good centre for the surrounding villages which were not served by the other market towns of Cambridge, Ely

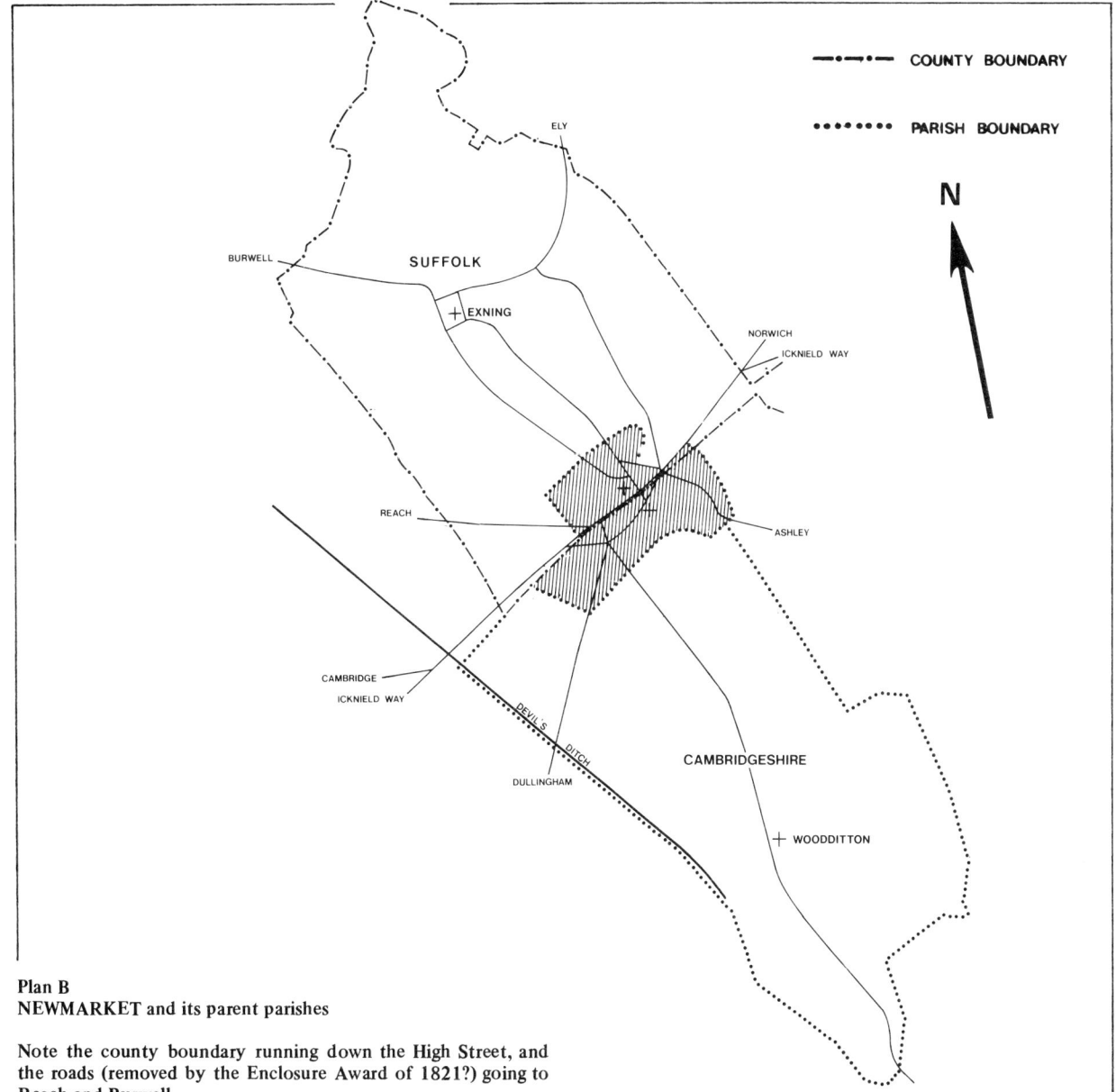

COUNTY BOUNDARY

PARISH BOUNDARY

N

ELY

SUFFOLK

BURWELL

EXNING

NORWICH
ICKNIELD WAY

REACH

ASHLEY

CAMBRIDGE
ICKNIELD WAY

DEVIL'S DITCH

DULLINGHAM

CAMBRIDGESHIRE

WOODDITTON

**Plan B**
**NEWMARKET** and its parent parishes

Note the county boundary running down the High Street, and
the roads (removed by the Enclosure Award of 1821?) going to
Reach and Burwell.

5

and Bury St Edmunds — markets at Worlington (1258), Moulton (1298), Barrow (1267), Ousden (1254) and Mildenhall (1412) were all established later than that at Newmarket.[23] Moreover Newmarket lies in a slight dip, as the contour figures show, with the water-course running through the dip and so providing the necessary water supply. What more fitting place could be found for a market to grow up more or less spontaneously? On the other hand Richard Argentein may have been a shrewd businessman, seen the potential of his marriage portion, and, as a financial speculation, deliberately developed his market and town.

It is apparently characteristic of new towns that they appear on the map like small bites of the piece of bread that is their parent parish; this is transparently true of Newmarket and its two parent parishes of Exning and Woodditton (see plan B on page 5). In the 19th century Exning's acreage was 5710, Woodditton's 4899, and the whole of Newmarket, corresponding to the old wards of St Mary's and All Saints', was only 570 acres, not much more than a twentieth of the parent parishes. On the other hand it might be argued that the size and shape of Newmarket could have been determined by the fact that this was the size and shape of Cassandra's marriage portion.

A 15th century document shows ten tenements lying between Black Bear Lane and Church Lane, all more or less of the same size — you can identify these tenements today if you walk round the block bounded by these roads and Fitzroy Street and the High Street.[24] This would suggest some measure of planning. But if Newmarket was a planned town, we would expect to find standard rents for these more or less equal tenements; in fact they vary from as much as 6s 1d to as little as 2d. Moreover the occupants of at least two of these tenements were not tenants of the lord of the manor. This suggests a much more natural and haphazard growth of the town round the market.

Thus although there is a case for Newmarket being a planned town, deliberately laid out by Richard Argentein, it seems more likely that it grew up more naturally along a busy medieval highway. Either alternative in any case is preferable to the tradition that the market at Exning was transferred to Newmarket because of a plague.

We have now discussed fairly fully the origins of Newmarket at the end of the 12th and the beginning of the 13th century. In our next chapter we must go on to consider the ways in which it developed.

## Chapter Two

## THE CHARACTER OF THE NEW TOWN

It has been estimated that between the years 1227 and 1350 some twelve hundred places in England and Wales were granted charters to hold markets, and most of them became market towns.[1] Although Newmarket had its origin a few years earlier, it is therefore one of a goodly company of similar places.

Before looking at the character of the new market town of Newmarket, we may note two points of importance. First the rise of these market towns marks a development in the way in which the social and economic life of our country was organised. Generally speaking, up to this time England had consisted of villages like Exning and Woodditton and of towns and county boroughs like London, Norwich, Cambridge and Bury St Edmunds. But even in the time of the Domesday Book some villages such as Clare and Stowmarket had become minor market centres to which villagers could bring their produce and at which they could purchase what they themselves could not produce. In the creation of so many market towns between 1227 and 1350, we see not something completely new but the acceleration and development of something that already existed in embryo. The second point of importance arises from this. To the average citizen in the 20th century a market means very little, but in the later middle ages market day was the centre of the villager's week, the day he could take his goods to sell and buy himself what he needed. The medieval market stall was not so much a store as a workshop, in which the trader sat and made there and then what was ordered of him. These two points must be borne in mind as we look at the character of our new market town.

We propose to do this by comparing the manor of Newmarket with one of the manors of Exning; there were three manors in Exning, Valence or Cotton, Well Hall or Coggeshall and Jarden's or Gardener's.[2] Fortunately for us a lord of the manor of Well Hall, Edmund Kemesek, died more or less at the same time as a lord of the manor of Newmarket, Sir Giles Argentein; and we have surveys of the contents of Edmund's manor for 1288 and Sir Giles' for 1283.[3] We shall more easily note the changes involved in the development of a new market town from a village economy, and at the same time obtain a picture of Newmarket at the end of the 13th century, by putting these two surveys in parallel columns and commenting on various items.

| | Sir Giles Argentein of Newmarket (1283) | Edmund Kemesek of Exning (1288) |
|---|---|---|
| 1 | | A capital messuage valued at 12d per annum |
| 2 | 76 acres of arable land valued at 4d an acre | 180 acres of arable land valued at 4d an acre |
| 3 | | 3 acres of meadow valued at 8d an acre |
| 4 | | 6¼ acres of pasture land valued at 3d an acre |
| 5 | A windmill valued at £2 a year | A windmill valued at 10s a year |
| 6 | | A dovecot valued at 2s a year |
| 7 | 'Rent of assize' of freemen valued at £3 9s a year | 'Rent of assize' of freemen and customary tenants valued at £6 1s 1d a year |
| 8 | | 741 'winter works' by customary tenants valued at £1 10s 10½d |
| 9 | | 574 'boon works' by customary tenants valued at £1 15s 9d |
| 10 | | 20 'boon works' by 2 'cottars' valued at 2s 6d |
| 11 | | 4 cartloads of turves supplied by the same 2 'cottars' valued at 16d |
| 12 | A weekly market valued at £5 a year | |
| 13 | The advowson of a chapel | |

**Illustration 1**                       **Fifteenth century travellers**

First we shall notice that Edmund Kemesek had a *capital messuage* in his manor, while Giles Argentein had not. The capital messuage was the main house of the lord of the manor in which he or his representative lived and from which the affairs of the manor were conducted; Edmund Kemesek had four other manors and we do not know whether he himself lived at Exning. Sir Giles Argentein was lord of several other manors besides Newmarket, notably Halesworth in Suffolk, Great Wymondley in Hertfordshire and Melbourn in Cambridgeshire.[4] His property in all of these three places was more extensive than in Newmarket and in each he had a capital messuage. The evidence seems to suggest that the Argenteins entrusted the management of their Newmarket manor to a bailiff, who was generally a local man. The steward who would have been responsible for overall manorial business appears to have lived outside Newmarket (in the early 15th century he was William Cheveley, presumably from the village of that name), and to have turned up every now and then to preside over one of the manorial courts. Although later account rolls record payments of sums of money 'in expenses of the lord coming to Newmarket on various occasions', we have to admit that the Argenteins and their successors, the Alingtons, were absentee lords of the manor.

The next item in the survey of Edmund Kemesek's Exning manor is 180 acres of arable land worth 4d an acre; Giles Argentein had only 76; in addition Edmund had 3 acres of meadow and 6½ acres of pasture land. These items, coupled with the reference to 'winter works' and 'boon works' in the survey of Exning, give us another clue to the character of the Argentein manor of Newmarket. On long-standing manors, like Edmund Kemesek's, there was a ready supply of conscript labour in the form of villeins or serfs living on the manor, called customary tenants; these tenants had to give so many days' work on the lord's fields every week — they were called customary because they had been on the manor by long-standing custom since Domesday and beyond. 'Winter works' were to be done from Michaelmas Day (29 September) until Lammas Day (1 August); 'boon works' were works additional to these which had to be given especially during harvest (from 1 August until Michaelmas Day), and at any peak period of work. To give an example from the manor of Ditton Valens, the Woodditton manor most closely associated with Newmarket, in 1300 there were seventeen customary tenants, of two sorts, major tenants with seven or more acres of land, and minor tenants with two or three acres of land or less. Each of these seventeen tenants had to give one day's work a week to the lord of the manor. They could be allotted almost any kind of work on the manor, from hedging the lord's woods to scattering 'muck', from cleaning out the dovecot to making hurdles for the sheepfold. As for 'boon works' at harvest time, each of the eleven major tenants had to reap half an acre every Monday, and a rood every Tuesday, Thursday and Friday, while each of the minor tenants, occupying less manorial land, had to reap only half an acre every Monday. There was also one 'cottar', possibly a smallholder or craftsman, who had to reap a rood every Monday. They were all excused 'works' on Saints' Days, holy days that were really holidays! In this way all the 120 acres of manorial land on the Ditton Valens manor were reaped, bound and gathered.[5] In a somewhat similar way Edmund Kemesek would have got the work on his manor done by his customary tenants and two cottars. Giles' grandfather, Richard Argentein, the possible founder of Newmarket, would not have found a ready-made labour force to hand, and no freeman would have been willing to accept the terms on which the customary tenants worked on Edmund Kemesek's land; Richard would have had to make other arrangements for working his arable fields.

Later, in the 15th century, lords of the Newmarket manor did two things with their arable fields. They 'farmed out' about half of their acres, that is they leased them to the highest bidder for a period of years, at an annual rent, with no strings attached. The other half they rented out, at a fixed rent (for this is what 'rent of assize' appears to mean) to tenants who could dispose of their acres as they wished, always of course with the lord's permission and at a fee. Such tenants were required to pay 'suit of court', that is to attend the manorial courts (called General Courts) held twice a year to deal with

**Illustration 2**    **A fifteenth century town official**

Notice his yardstick and, on his shoulder, his standard pot, with which to check measures, also his purse for collecting tolls and rents, and his keys.

the business of the manor.[6] In the absence of the kind of conscript labour that Edmund Kemesek could command at Exning, it seems likely that Giles Argentein will have worked his fields in the 13th century in much the same way as his 15th century successors.

Here then is a major difference between those who lived on the Well Hall manor at Exning (and indeed on most village manors) and those who lived on the Argentein manor at Newmarket. The latter were probably all free tenants, even though they had not many acres to farm, and certainly self-employed, while the former were clearly for the most part unfree villeins very much at the mercy of the lords of Well Hall manor.

Although our survey for Sir Giles Argentein's Newmarket manor does not include any meadow, we know that later lords of the manor held ten acres of meadow called 'Lord's Meadow' (see plan E on page 39), the hay from which they sold at 4s an acre; meadow was much more valuable than arable because it provided the very necessary fodder for cattle during the hard winter

months. Sir Giles may have made the same arrangements about the hay from his meadow (perhaps accidentally omitted from the survey), but at all events what is clear from all this is that the Argenteins saw their acres of land as a financial investment rather than as a means of supplying provisions for their own table. Here then is another possible difference between the two manors. Edmund Kemesek will have seen his land first and foremost as a means of providing his own table, and then secondly, by sending the surplus to market, as a source of financial profit.

It is in place here to say something about the 'Fields' of Exning and the 'Field' of Newmarket. Later documents show that Exning had seven large fields, of probably 200 acres each; going clockwise round the village they were South Field (later divided into Little South Field and Great South Field), West Field, Windmill Field, Harborough Field, Arnold Field, East Field and Brakenden Field. Brakenden Field straddled the roads between Newmarket and Exning; its name suggests that it had been waste land 'broken' or brought under cultivation in the comparatively recent past. These were the common fields of Exning in the 17th century and it is very likely that they were the same in the 13th. They were divided into strips of all sizes, distributed among the various tenants and inhabitants of the manor. They were subjected to a common course of agriculture by which some fields would lie fallow each year while the other fields were cultivated. Since the strips of each individual tenant were scattered among the different fields, he had always at least some strips under cultivation. Clearly Exning, with these seven large fields, had an agriculturally based economy.

In contrast Newmarket had only one 'Field', of 182 acres, called in 1633 Market Means (see plan E on page 39). A 15th century document tells us about this field thus:

The saide Felde of Newmarket is severede frome the Feldes of Yxnyng be usyng and ocupyng. For the Feldes of Yxnyng ar too yeres dowen and the thirde yere ly valowe [fallow]. Ande the felde of Newmarket is every yere dowen. Ande whan upon ther is Chirche

Halydaye in Yxnyng they Forbere alle werkes withyn ther towne and feldes than in Newmarket Felde they kepe ther ocupacion with the plowe ande with ther labor etc.[7]

Such statements smack of antiquity, and it may well have been the same 200 years earlier. But in any case it will be clear from this that Newmarket was not agriculturally based like Exning. The fact that Newmarket folk worked in their common field on holydays does not mean that they were less religious than Exning folk; it simply means that they were free men, or, as we should say today, self-employed, free to work when and how they liked, and not at the beck and call of a lord of the manor. It may also indicate that their main interests were in the crafts and commerce from which they would be free on holy days to work on their land.

Both Edmund Kemesek and Giles Argentein had windmills. A windmill was a profitable source of income for a lord of a manor, because he normally insisted, at a fee, on his tenants grinding their corn at *his* mill and nowhere else. The Newmarket mill was at the top of Exning Road, Millhill being of course the hill leading to the mill, and Millbank on Freshfields being a reminder to us in the 20th century of its siting in the past. The other Newmarket windmill was on the Cambridgeshire side of the town, where 'Little Murray' now is, and was in the Ditton Valens manor of Woodditton. Edmund Kemesek's manor seems to have been near Landwade, but where the windmill was is uncertain, perhaps on the present Windmill Hill. It is perhaps curious that Giles Argentein, with much less arable land than Edmund Kemesek, got more income from his mill; perhaps he insisted that all corn bought or sold in his market was ground there.

Both Edmund Kemesek and Giles Argentein received income from 'rent of assize', that is from land and tenements let out at a fixed rent to tenants who could dispose of them, with the lord's permission and at a fine, as they wished. What is important to note is that Giles' rent of assize came from free men, while Edmund's came from both free men and customary tenants, the latter being the villeins to whom we have already referred. Again we are seeing a radical difference between those who lived

in the old village agricultural manor of Exning and those who lived in the new market town of Newmarket; this difference is underlined, as we have already seen, by the mention of 'winter works' and 'boon works'. We may note that there was a third type of tenant on Edmund's manor, namely two 'cottars', who like the villeins were conscripted to do 'boon works' and had an additional chore, that of cutting and carting two cartloads of turf or peat a year, presumably from the fen adjoining Well Hall manor. Cottars were smallholders, sometimes craftsmen, of higher or lower standing than villeins, but lower than freemen.

Fifteenth century account rolls show that the Argenteins' rent of assize (or fixed rents) came from two sources, from land and from tenements or holdings. According to these rolls there were some fifty such holdings, forty-five of which were situated down either side of the High Street. There were twenty-six on the northern side of the High Street, from the present Black Bear Lane to the Clock Tower, and nineteen on the southern side from the Rutland Arms (then the Ram) to 'Dundich', presumably the water course where it runs today under the Jockey Club buildings (see plan D on pages 32—33). These rolls also record that there were ten holdings between Black Bear Lane and Church Lane: John Chapman's *Plan of the Town of Newmarket* (dated 1787) shows quite clearly these ten holdings, abutting on the High Street to the south and on what is now Fitzroy Street to the north (see plan C on page 12). They can still be identified today by walking round the block enclosed by Church Lane, St Mary's Church, Fitzroy Street, Black Bear Lane and the High Street. We cannot of course be sure that these were the same holdings rented out by Sir Giles Argentein in the 13th century, but we can at least be certain that the pattern of holdings down either side of the High Street was set very early in the life of the manor.

The letting of land and holdings at fixed rents was later to prove an embarrassment to lords of the manor in times of inflation such as occurred in the 16th century; they seem to have overcome this to some extent by increasing the amount of fee due on entry into a tenancy.

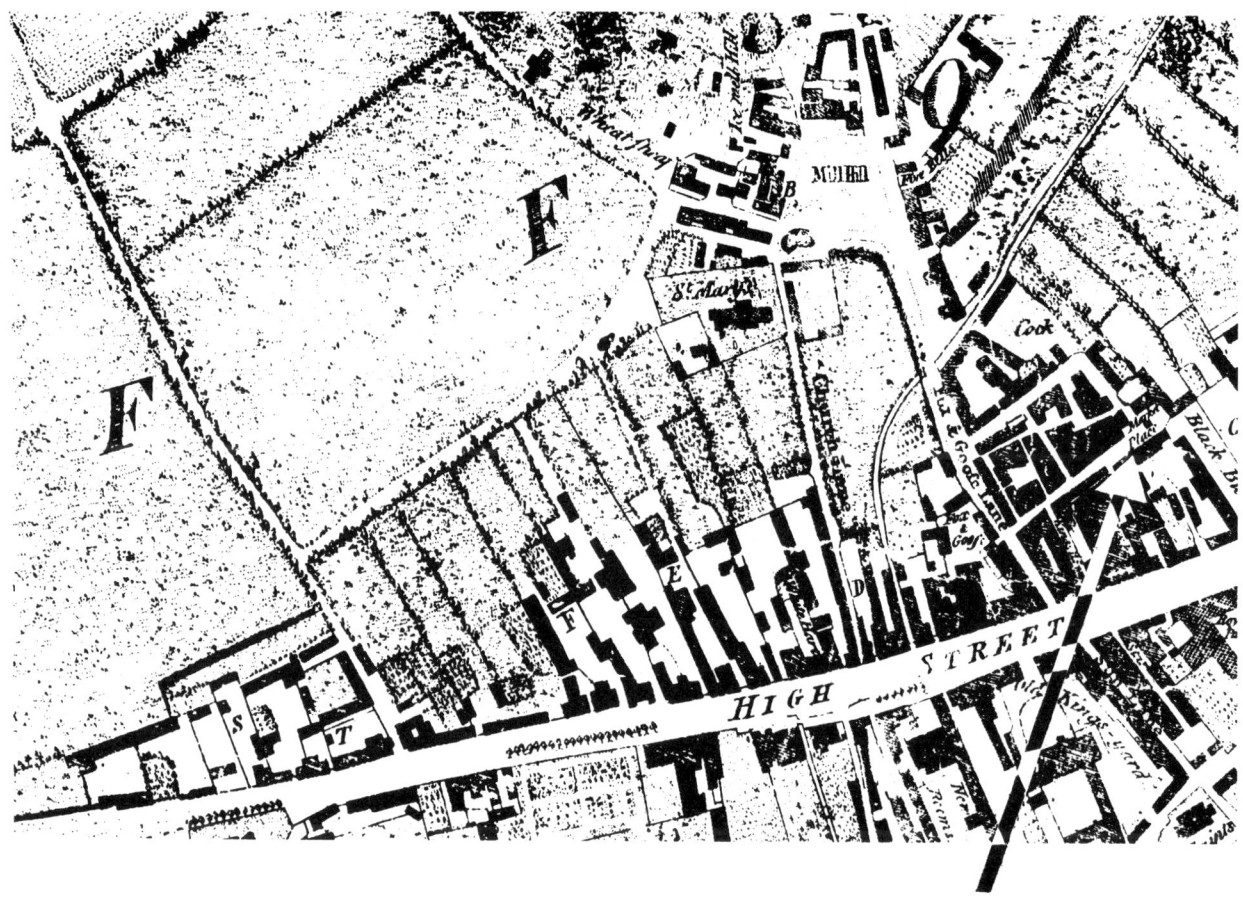

Plan C
A section of John Chapman's *Plan of Newmarket*, dated 1787, showing St Mary's Church, the open field (Market Means) lying north of what is now Fitzroy Street, and the boundaries of the ten 15th century holdings between Church Lane and the present Black Bear Lane.

Note also the tiny Market Place, and the rectangle of buildings to its west where the 15th century market was sited before encroachment took place. The small building between the words 'Market' and 'Place' may well be the Tollbooth (see page 29).

12

Next we notice that the highest source of income on the Argentein manor was the market, a source of income denied to Edmund Kemesek who had no market. The obvious conclusion of course is that Newmarket's economy, even in these early days, as its name implies, was market based and not agriculturally based like its parent parish Exning. We shall look at the market in some detail in a later chapter. Here it is sufficient to point out that the cigar-shaped bulge in the High Street suggests that originally the market was probably held in the High Street itself in the 13th century; as we shall see, by the 15th century it had been transferred to the Rookery area, more or less where it is today.

Finally we note that Giles Argentein had what Edmund Kemesek had not, the advowson of a chapel on his manor. The advowson of St Martin's Church, Exning, was in the hands of the Abbot of Battle Abbey in Kent; ecclesiastically the St Mary's side of Newmarket remained within Exning parish until the 16th century, and Giles' chapel was a chapel of ease to that parish. Since an early survey of 1265 does not mention any advowson, we may perhaps assume that Giles himself had the chapel built, sometime between 1265 and 1283, as one account says 'for the health of the souls of his ancestors'.[8] It has been noted that chapels were often built in the middle ages to serve market based communities living at some distance from their parish church.[9] Giles Argentein may therefore have built his chapel not only as an act of piety for his ancestors but also for the good of his market town. He or one of his successors as lord of the manor seems also to have made some provision for its endowment; for at the beginning of the 15th century a tenth of the proceeds of the annual fair, probably because it was held in St Mary's Square, was paid over to 'the guardian of the old chapel of the blessed Mary' as its parish priest was called. The rapid development of Newmarket at the expense of Exning also meant that its residents would wish their chapel of ease to become a parish church in its own right, independent of its mother church at Exning. Hence by 1633 the St Mary's parson had forty-three pieces of land as his glebe, mostly under an acre each, scattered over the fields of Exning, Woodditton and Newmarket, indicating that endowment had been going on apace in the earlier years.[10] In the 15th century every 'stranger' taking gravel, sand or chalk from the Millhill had to pay 1d a load to St Mary's Church, and half the fines for illegal gleaning went 'for the work of the church'.[11] By 1538 it is no longer being called the chapel of the blessed Mary but the parish church of Newmarket.[12]

One curious omission from the survey of Sir Giles Argentein's Newmarket manor in 1283 is the annual fair. It will be remembered that although we have no charter for the establishment of the market, King Henry III's charter of 1223 granting Richard Argentein the right to hold a fair has survived. Reginald, Giles' son and heir, when examined in 1287 about his manorial rights, claimed among other things that his ancestors had been granted a fair, and his claim was admitted by the king's representative who was making the examination.[13] In fact in 1293 Reginald obtained from King Edward II a charter to hold a *second* fair, on the three days around St Barnabas' Day (11 June).[14] This was known later as the 'Petyaistomin' (or Little Summer) Fair, and was evidently smaller than that held around St Simon and St Jude's Day (28 October). The two fairs were no doubt held in St Mary's Square, frequently called Fairstead in later documents (see plan E on page 39).

When Reginald Argentein was examined in 1287, he also claimed, as also did Edmund Kemesek (he was still alive), that he had the right to erect a gallows and hang criminals caught within his manor. Every lord of the manor wanted more authority and power to his arm within his own manorial territory, and especially at this time was striving to assert his own rights over against the king's. The right to hang a criminal carried with it the right to take to himself his goods and chattels. King Edward I was determined to curb the powers of manorial lords, and to assert that he alone, through his royal coroners in each county, had the power to erect gallows and hang criminals. He was strong enough to do this, and Reginald's and Edmund's claims 'to have the gallows' on their manors were rejected by the king's representatives.

Reginald and Edmund made two other claims as lords of their manors in 1287, namely that they had what was

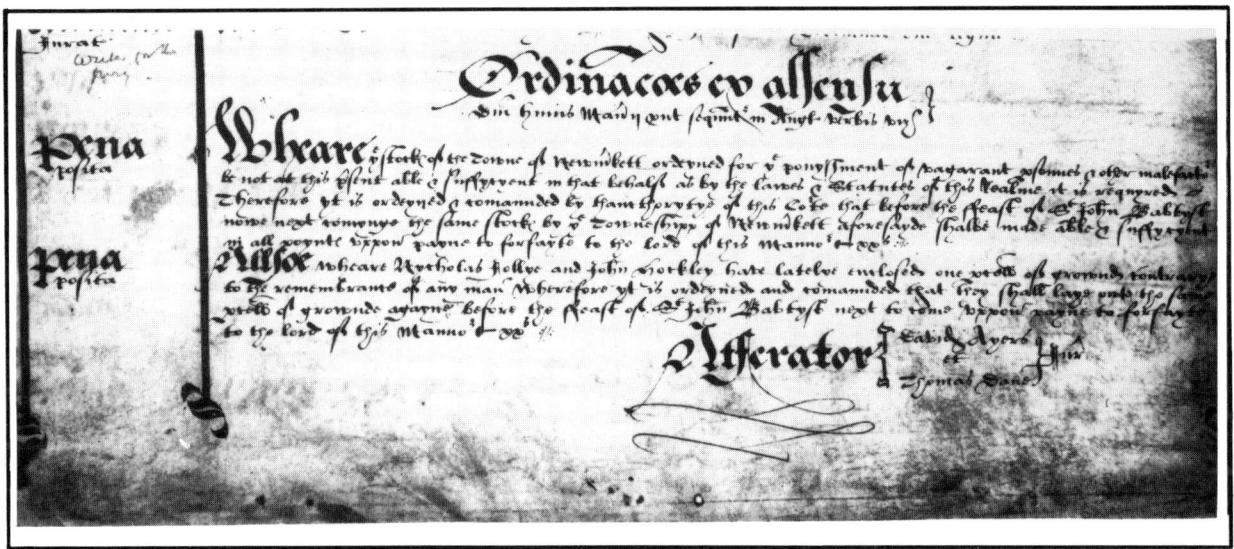

**Illustration 3**
An Order to repair the stocks at Newmarket, made at the Leet or View of Frankpledge in 1580

The second item orders Nicholas Jollye and John Hockley to restore to communal use a piece of land which they had enclosed.

called the View of Frankpledge and the right to take for themselves the fines arising out of the regulations controlling the making and sale of bread and ale. In regard to the View of Frankpledge the sheriff of Suffolk came on 1 August every year to Exning and Newmarket, to examine, among other matters, the way in which the inhabitants had behaved during the past year in maintaining the king's peace; this court of enquiry was called the View of Frankpledge. Richard Argentein, when his charter for a fair was confirmed in 1227, had received the right to receive the fines imposed by the sheriff at the Newmarket View of Frankpledge for breaches of the peace. Breaches of the regulations for the making and sale of bread and ale did not come under the purview of the View of Frankpledge, at least not in Newmarket.

This meant that Richard had the right to establish his own court to fine people for breaking these and other manorial regulations. In Newmarket this court was called the General Court — elsewhere it was sometimes called the Court Baron; all tenants of the manor had to attend this court which was held twice a year.

Reginald's claim to have the View of Frankpledge and the fines from breaches of the regulations for the making and sale of bread and ale was accepted by the king's representatives without question. When Edmund Kemesek's Exning tenants were examined about his claims, they stated that Edmund held his own court a few days before the sheriff arrived, took the fines for breaches of the king's peace, and then proceeded to take them a second time when the sheriff came on 1 August for the View of

Frankpledge! A timely bribe of 100s and the promise not to hold his own earlier court again enabled Edmund to escape any more dire consequences.

It has been argued that fairs and markets were occasions not only for the selling and buying of goods but also gave people attending them the opportunity to settle disputes and debts.[15] This second purpose of fairs and markets was attained by having special fair courts and market courts meeting on the actual days of the fairs and markets. Certainly by 1400 the lords of the manor of Newmarket had their twice-yearly fair courts, and, at least in theory, weekly market courts, as well as the annual View of Frankpledge or Leet as it was called in Newmarket, and their twice-yearly General Courts.

We have called 13th century Newmarket a market town, but in effect it was little more than a village with a market. What made it different from the average village like its two parent parishes, Exning and Woodditton, were several factors. First its population was made up largely of free men and not of villeins. Secondly its economy was market based and not agriculturally based. Thirdly it was minute in size compared with the average village — we have to remember that it corresponded so far as we can judge to the old St Mary's Ward with a small overspill on to the Cambridgeshire side of the High Street, corresponding to the old All Saints' Ward. Fourthly it was ideally situated on the great London to Norwich road, and at the centre of roads branching off in several directions. This last factor does not emerge from the surveys which we have been examining in this chapter, but it is a factor which runs through the whole of its history, and it is this factor, together with the heath which surrounds it, which has made Newmarket so very much more than a small market town.

Illustration 4
Fifteenth century
market stalls

16

## Chapter Three

## THE WIDER WORLD

Until the 17th century when King James I found Newmarket a suitable venue for the hunting of hares and for falconry, Newmarket can claim no distinguished man of the wider world. Although important people no doubt passed through it on their journeys between London and Norwich, until the 17th century there was nothing in Newmarket to encourage them to linger. The only real link with the outside world of England seems to have been their lords of the manor, at first the Argenteins and then later the Alingtons, and even they, as we have seen, were absentee landlords. Nonetheless, since they were an important part of the Newmarket scene, we shall summarise what we know of the two families who held the manor of Newmarket from its founding until the middle of the 18th century.[1]

### Lords of the Manor

Members of the Argentein family were lords of the manor of Newmarket from its founding at the beginning of the 13th century until John Argentein died without issue in 1413, leaving his manor to his two sisters, Elizabeth and Joan. They married two brothers, William and Robert Alington respectively, and members of the Alington family were lords of the manor until the middle of the 18th century.

There appear to have been two main reasons why the Argentein family, while drawing regular revenue from their Newmarket manor, were absentee landlords. The first reason is that for a century or more after the founding of Newmarket they were busy with affairs of state. Richard, who, as we have seen, is generally regarded as

the founder, was for example sheriff at one time or another of four East Anglian counties (Cambridgeshire, Huntingdonshire, Essex and Hertfordshire), governor of Hertford Castle and one of the stewards of King Henry III's household.[2]

He was succeeded on his death in 1246 by Giles — we looked at the 1283 survey of his Newmarket manor in our last chapter. Giles was involved in two of King Henry III's expeditions, into Wales in 1231, and ten years later into Gascony, and was governor of Windsor Castle in 1242.[3] When Simon de Montfort, Earl of Leicester, rebelled against the King in 1264, Giles joined him and, in a 17th century historian's words, 'was elected one of the nine Counsellors by whom the Realm should be governed'; in this capacity his signature was on many of the decrees passed by the rebel government. The rebels were however defeated at the battle of Evesham in August 1265, and all Giles' lands, including his Newmarket manor, were confiscated. Eventually he and his son Reginald were pardoned, and when he died in 1283 he was in possession of his Newmarket manor again. Incidentally, during the confiscation the rents were collected by William de Desenige, the Domesday name for Gazeley, a name still retained in Desning Hall in that village.[4]

Giles' son, Reginald, was the first Baron Argentein, and as such was summoned to Parliament as a member of the House of Lords; he was the last of the Argenteins to play a major part in the affairs of state. He died in 1307 and was succeeded by his son John, of whom more later. One of Reginald's sons, another Giles, a Knight Templar and a crusader, died gloriously at the battle of Bannockburn in 1314 when King Edward II was defeated by the Scots under Robert Bruce. Sir Walter Scott gives a vivid description of his death in *The Lord of the Isles*, and makes Robert Bruce press the dying hand of his former friend and fellow crusader, now his enemy, and cry out:

> Of chivalry the flower and pride,
> The arm in battle bold,
> The courteous mien, the noble race,
> The stainless faith, the manly face!

17

Bid Ninian's convent light their shrine,
For late-wake of de Argentine,
O'er better knight, on death-bier laid
Torch never gleam'd nor mass was said.[5]

Mention of the crusades reminds us that 13th century knights were not only busy on affairs of state in England; it was also the century of the crusades. Matthew Paris, the 13th century historian, describes the death of Richard Argentein in 1246 as a great national loss of one 'who had fought long for God in the Holy Land'.[6] He was apparently known as 'David's tower' because of his valour in battle,[7] and although Matthew Paris does not specifically say so, it is generally thought that he died while fighting against the Saracens before Antioch.

Another member of the family, a Reginald Argentein, who was not in fact lord of the manor, died in heroic circumstances at the battle of Darbesak near Antioch in 1237; in Matthew Paris' words:

There fell in that disastrous battle a famous Knight Templar, an Englishman, Reginald de Argenomio, who was standard bearer for the day; tirelessly he carried the standard until his hands and legs were broken and he was slain.[8]

The second reason why the Argenteins were absentee landlords from their Newmarket manor may have been bound up with the first. Their other manors were at Halesworth in Suffolk, at Great Wymondley in Hertfordshire and at Melbourn in Cambridgeshire. The latter two places were much nearer the centres of power and government than Halesworth and Newmarket; and it was at Great Wymondley and at Melbourn that the Argenteins set up their establishments.[9] Their coat of arms, three silver cups, derived from their responsibility, as lords of the manor of Great Wymondley, of offering a silver cup to the sovereign at his coronation banquet. Having established themselves and their families at Great Wymondley and Melbourn, the Argenteins did not do more than pay an occasional visit to Newmarket.

What made the manor of Newmarket even less important to the Argenteins was its division into two separate manors early in the 14th century. John Argentein, who succeeded Reginald on his death in 1307, had three daughters by his first wife Joan; one, Denise, died unmarried; the other two, Joan and Elizabeth, married two brothers, John le Botiller and William le Botiller, respectively. By his second wife Agnes, John Argentein had a son John who was only six months old when his father died in 1318. The manor of Newmarket was divided; the two daughters took half, called henceforward Butler's Manor, and the young John took the other half, still called Argentein Manor of Newmarket. As the Butlers seem to have lived at Norbury in Middlesex, they like the Argenteins were absentee landlords. The two manors were re-united in 1536, but in practice they had probably been operating as one manor since the division, for in the 1470s one bailiff acted in Newmarket for both, administering both manors and distributing the income according to the terms of the division.

Young John Argentein was lord of his half of the manor until his death in 1382. His grandson, another John, died in 1423 without male issue, and his two sisters, Elizabeth and Joan, inherited it. They married two brothers; Joan married Robert Alington of Horseheath in Cambridgeshire, and died at the age of eighteen in 1429, leaving two daughters. On her death her sister and co-heiress Elizabeth inherited the whole of the Argentein manor; she had married William Alington, also of Horseheath, Robert's older brother. Like the Argenteins the Alingtons were absentee landlords, and seemingly for the same reasons. William Alington died in 1459 and was succeeded by his son, another William; he was Speaker of the House of Commons and lived at Bottisham in Cambridgeshire, only a few miles from Newmarket. He is said to have given the stone screen in Bottisham church, and a stone tomb chest beside the pulpit is thought to be his. There is still today an Alington Hill leading to Hare Park off the A 11 at Bottisham. In 1479 he became a member of the Privy Council, but died later in the year.[10] Clearly he was too busy a man to interest himself very much in Newmarket.

William had no children, and so was succeeded by his brother John who had been sheriff of Cambridgeshire in 1461. John survived his older brother by only a year, and was succeeded by his son, another William, who was killed at the battle of Bosworth in 1485. William's son, Giles, died in 1522, and his son, another Giles, died in 1586, at the ripe old age of eighty-six, outliving both his son and his grandson as lord of the manors of Newmarket and Horseheath. The second Giles was a public figure, being High Sheriff of Cambridgeshire in 1530/31 and of Huntingdonshire in 1545/46, and, according to one authority, attended King Henry VIII as his Minister of Ordnance at the siege of Boulogne in 1545.[11]

Memorial inscriptions and impressive monuments to several of the Alingtons are to be seen in Horseheath church, an indication that this was their main seat; account rolls show that they only occasionally visited Newmarket.

Illustration 5
A fifteenth century taverner
offering food and drink to a traveller

## Tournaments at Newmarket

The King [Edward II] to his beloved and loyal Dukes, Barons, Knights and all other men-at-arms, about to meet for a tournament at Newmarket on this coming Sunday. We firmly forbid you, under penalty of forfeit of all that you possess, holding a tournament, jousting, seeking 'knightly adventures' or exercizing any feats of arms, without our licence, on that day, at Newmarket or elsewhere within our realm.[12]

So runs a mandate sent out from London on 17 January 1313, presumably in reference to the following Sunday, 21 January. Two people were appointed to enforce this prohibition and to arrest all persons disobeying the King's mandate – it was the last of several such mandates put out by the King in the period 1309–1313. Although addressed to *all* dukes, barons etc, the mandate expressly mentions seven men by name, including the Earl of Pembroke, the Earl of Gloucester and Hertford and the Earl of Surrey, all large local landowners.

The romantic picture that most of us have of knights jousting in armour and on horseback has to be modified by the fact that, although such tournaments were the only training ground for the contemporary arts of war, they often deteriorated into pitched battles between rival groups of bored young noblemen. Because of this, over 100 years earlier, King Richard II had allowed tournaments to be held in only five places in England (Newmarket was hardly in existence, so it was not one of the five). Moreover, short of money, he charged the five places concerned for the privilege of holding such tournaments, and those who took part had to pay, on a sliding scale according to their social standing, for participating.[13]

Edward II's prohibition of tournaments at Newmarket was not however to prevent pitched battles between bored young noblemen. It was rather to prevent rebellious barons from using the occasion of a tournament to band together against him. Presumably Newmarket would have been a suitable place for the barons concerned to meet. What is interesting from our point of view is that as early as the 14th century Newmarket Heath was seen to be a suitable place for massed events

19

spread over a wide area, similar *mutatis mutandis* to our 20th century race meetings.

## The Black Death of 1349

The Black Death seems to have reached England from the continent in the summer of 1348, somewhere on the south coast, perhaps at Southampton or at Weymouth. It arrived in East Anglia in March 1349 and raged there for the four months of May, June, July and August. The toll in lives over the whole of England was enormous; out of an estimated population of 4.2 millions, it is safe to say that between 25 per cent and 33 per cent died, over a million. The highest figure suggested by modern historians is 45 per cent and the lowest 23 per cent.[14] It is likely that the percentage of deaths in East Anglia was higher than the national average. Before we consider its impact on Newmarket, some preliminary remarks may be made.

First what was the Black Death? It now appears to be agreed that there were two main varieties of the plague that goes by this name. Bubonic plague, originating apparently in East Asia, was carried by flea-infested rats and was characterized by boils or tumours, called buboes, in the loin and the armpits. Pneumonic plague attacked the lungs and was spread by the cough of its victim; it was more infectious than bubonic plague. It seems likely that in some degree both played their part in the Black Death. Death from either variety seems to have been quick, sometimes immediate, but usually within three to five days. Our medieval forefathers had no remedy and no means of escape, and were so terrified that they often abandoned victims to their fate and made no attempt to help them.

Second why was it called the Black Death? It used to be said that it got its name because the flesh of the victims blackened; this explanation however is unlikely because the actual term 'the Black Death' was not used by contemporary writers — in fact the first recorded use of the term is said to be nearly 200 years later. Possibly the original latin *mors atra* or *pestis atra* was mistranslated — *atra* can mean both 'terrible' and 'black'. However

that may be, no one can deny that it is a singularly appropriate name for the devastating plague of 1349.

Nowadays in this 20th century it would be easy to work out statistics to determine the effects of such a plague not only in England in general but in East Anglia in particular. In the 14th century few records were kept and many of the documentary sources from which we might obtain the relevant information have disappeared with time. One method which has been used is to compare the numbers of clergy instituted to parish livings in the year from 25 March 1349 to 25 March 1350 with the numbers instituted in normal years. Since Newmarket is on the borders of Cambridgeshire and Suffolk, our concern is with the two dioceses of Norwich and Ely, whose ecclesiastical jurisdiction covered these two counties.[15] According to one authority

> In the years before the Black Death the average annual figure for episcopal institutiohs [in the diocese of Norwich] was eighty-one. In the year between 25 March 1349 and 25 March 1350 the total rose to 831,

over ten times as many.[16] With a previous monthly average of just under seven, in June 1349 there were 110 institutions, in July over 190 and in August over 130. In the diocese of Ely (a much smaller diocese) there were five institutions in a normal year; there were no less than ninety-two in the relevant year of 1349/50, eighteen times as many as normal; in June there were seventeen, in July twenty-five and in August twelve.[17] As institutions were made in medieval England almost as soon as a vacancy occurred, it seems clear that the plague was most virulent in our part of East Anglia in June, July and August, at its peak in July. The diocese of Norwich shares with the dioceses of Exeter and Winchester the doubtful privilege of having the highest percentage (48.8 per cent) of deathrate among parish priests in England in the year concerned, followed closely by the diocese of Ely with 48.5 per cent.[18] Although clearly we must not assume that all these vacancies were caused by plague deaths, it is obvious that a very large percentage of parish priests in our two dioceses of Norwich and Ely died as a result of the Black Death. Parish priests, with their responsibilities for visiting the sick, hearing the confessions of the dying and burying the dead, were possibly at greater risk than other people, and therefore it is difficult to use these statistics to estimate the deathrate of ordinary people, but they certainly suggest that in East Anglia it must have been well above the national average.

Just as the deathrate among clergy varied from diocese to diocese, so also it varied from deanery to deanery and from parish to parish. For example the percentage of deaths in the Thingoe deanery (which included Bury St Edmunds) was only 26 per cent, but in Fordham deanery (which included Newmarket, Exning and Woodditton) it was 48 per cent, and in Clare deanery (which included Moulton, Gazeley and Dalham) it was 50 per cent.[19] The incidence of clergy deaths within the deaneries suggests that the plague was more virulent in some parishes than in others. For example there were no institutions at Ousden, Lidgate, Stradishall and Wickhambrook; were these villages untouched by the plague (yet there was one in the neighbouring village of Cowlinge)? In Little Thurlow there were two institutions (in May and September) and so too in Little Bradley (in May and November) and one in Great Thurlow (though none in Great Bradley); were these villages decimated by the plague? In Gazeley there were two (in June and July) and one each in Dalham, Kirtling and Moulton, but none in Ashley or Silverley. Of the parishes in the Ely diocese around Newmarket, Snailwell had two (in June and September), while Burwell, Swaffham Bulbeck, Bottisham, Quy, Stow, Westley Waterless, Dullingham and Stetchworth had one each.

Newmarket then, if we are to assume that most of the deaths of the parish priests in the neighbourhood were due to the plague, looks to have been in the very centre of it; yet there is no record of an institution at Newmarket St Mary's in the relevant year, nor was there one at either of the parent parishes of Exning and Woodditton.

Another source of information for the loss of life through the Black Death is the manorial court rolls which record the fines payable to the lord of the manor on the death of his tenants. Unfortunately none survive for the manors of Newmarket and Exning but we have the rolls for the manor of Ditton Valens (the Woodditton manor

holding the All Saints' side of Newmarket) and these are most revealing. At the court held next after the year of the Black Death, in November 1351, the lord of the manor of Ditton Valens 'retained in his hands' (as the phrase went) the holdings of no less than eight out of his eighteen tenants 'because no heir came to claim them'. In other words the Black Death had completely obliterated eight households out of eighteen, nearly half the village. In two other cases the heir refused to take up the holding he had inherited, and in two others the heir was too young to take over.[20] Clearly the manor of Ditton Valens, so closely involved with Newmarket, was badly affected by the Black Death, and it seems unlikely that the rest of Newmarket escaped unscathed.

There were other effects besides death. One very obvious one was the shortage of labour to work the land: 'many crops', wrote a contemporary, 'rotted in the fields for lack of men to gather them'. With that went a rise in the rate a man could demand for his labour, and the refusal to accept a tenancy loaded with traditional 'winter' and 'boon works'; the two holdings refused by the heirs at Ditton Valens were finally let out on completely different terms. There was also 'a great cheapness of all things', so that 'a horse that was formerly worth 40s could be had for half a mark [6s 8d], . . . a sheep for 3d, a lamb for 2d.'[21] In February 1351 King Edward III took drastic steps in the Statute of Labourers to enforce a policy of wage restraint, requiring all labourers and craftsmen to work at pre-Black Death rates, and villeins to remain under the same conditions of tenancy with their lords, and neither seek service elsewhere nor become vagrants.[22]

The long term effects of the Black Death seem to have been a growing discontent among the ordinary labourers and craftsmen at the terms and conditions under which they worked, a discontent that was fanned by minor plagues in 1361 and 1374–75, and erupted finally in the Peasants' Revolt of 1381. Since that revolt seems to have been more violent in East Anglia than elsewhere we may perhaps surmise that the discontent consequent upon the Black Death was more widespread and deeply seated there than in other parts of England.

## Felonies on Newmarket Heath

The Heath may have been a suitable place for medieval tournaments; it was also a dangerous spot for travellers. In 1356 the sheriffs of Cambridgeshire and Suffolk were ordered to make enquiries

> touching grievous complaints that large numbers of felons and evildoers form unlawful assemblies and roam about on Newmarket Heath and the vicinage, hold the passes there and commit innumerable homicides, robberies and other misdeeds on those passing through those parts.[23]

The Patent Rolls record several pardons granted to such self-confessed highwaymen. For example William Wakkyng, commonly called 'Bedel', of London, confessed to having robbed, with four others, in October 1371, sixteen 'fyssheres' of 100s in gold and silver on 'le Newemarketheth'.[24] Another highwayman, who was committed in 1418 to Newgate with his concubine for frequenting the Heath and robbing and 'despoiling many of the king's subjects' was William Cratfield, a former rector of Wortham Eastgate in Suffolk.[25] We can picture the gaps in the Devil's Ditch with the woods around as being likely spots for the activities of such highwaymen; and perhaps these activities are the origin of the story that bookmakers travelling by train to Newmarket in the old days used to raise their hats as it passed through the gap in the Ditch.

Evidently the Heath continued to be a danger spot for travellers throughout our period. The Elizabethan satirist, Thomas Nashe, who was born at Lowestoft in 1567 and whose father was rector of West Harling in Norfolk, clearly knew the Heath to be notorious for highwaymen; no doubt he had often travelled across it on his way from Norwich to London. In 1592 he wrote:

> Thanks be to God I am *vacuus viator* [an empty handed traveller] and care not though I meet the Commissioners of Newmarket Heath [responsible for arresting highwaymen] at high midnight for any crosses, images, or pictures that I carry about me more than needs.[26]

Some fifty years later a party of twenty-two seamen were marching to London to join their ship, when one of them was shot and killed by an Irishman on horseback. The county sheriffs were recorded as being somewhat lacking in enthusiasm for 'apprehending of the murderers'.[27]

Another incident which reflects the dangerous nature of the Newmarket countryside occurred in 1382 when the prior of Wymondley (the site of one of the Argentein manors) was on his way to the funeral of Sir John Argentein at Halesworth. He was attacked by a crowd on Newmarket Heath, near Badlingham, and forced to give up the keys of a chest, containing various manorial documents, to William Argentein, an illegitimate son of Sir John, who was contesting the inheritance with Sir John's three legitimate daughters.[28] This incident may perhaps be bound up with the Peasants' Revolt of 1381 if only because it indicates the disturbed state of East Anglia at this time.

## The Peasants' Revolt of 1381

The so-called Peasants' Revolt of 1381 under Wat Tyler and Jack Straw, beginning in Kent, erupted into violence and disorder in London during the three days 13–15 June 1381. East Anglia was immediately involved, and it became so violent there that the historian R.B. Dobson can state:

> For periods of between a weekend and a fortnight much of East Anglia was plunged into a state of near anarchy.... Although it would be an exaggeration to claim that the whole of Eastern England was affected by the risings, it does seem to be the case that in June 1381 Norfolk, Suffolk and even Cambridgeshire were on the verge of experiencing a general revolution.[29]

Newmarket lies almost equidistant between the two main centres of the revolt in East Anglia, Cambridge and Bury St Edmunds, and no doubt was affected by this fact. In these two towns however it is clearly a misnomer to call it the *Peasants'* Revolt. In fact the burgesses of both towns seem to have been in alliance with peasants from outlying villages to attack wealthy ecclesiastical bodies, in particular Corpus Christi College in Cambridge and the great Benedictine abbey in Bury St Edmunds.

Under the leadership of John Wray, described by a contemporary as 'a most wicked priest', 50,000 men are said to have run wild in Bury St Edmunds, where they captured and beheaded the Lord Chief Justice, Lord John Cavendish. The prior of the abbey, John of Cambridge, whose gifts seem to have been musical rather than military, fled, was discovered in a wood near Newmarket, and after a mock trial was beheaded at Mildenhall. Because the burgesses of Bury St Edmunds were involved, Bury St Edmunds (as well as Cambridge) was one of the six towns exempted from the general amnesty declared in 1382, and had to pay the large fine of 2000 marks (over a thousand pounds).

There is no evidence of any Newmarket people taking part in the actual revolt, perhaps because they were for the most part free men and not villeins, and not affected much by ecclesiastical issues. But records of the courts held after the revolt show that men from the villages round Newmarket were heavily involved. The main leader seems to have been John Greystone of Bottisham who was duly beheaded. Most of the other leaders in the district, for example John Saffrey of Stow-cum-Quy, John Clement of Quy, John Wallingford of Weston Colville, John Kempe of Dullingham, Thomas Roode of Woodditton, Robert Turveye of Brinkley, William Cobbe of Gazeley and John Noble of Freckenham, were never captured and their goods and property were confiscated. It is often said that the main object of the Peasants' Revolt was to destroy the rolls (called customaries) in which the lords of the manors recorded the feudal obligations of the villeins on their manors. This does not seem to have been the case in the Newmarket area. Those active in the surrounding villages appear to have been more concerned to loot the premises of the wealthier inhabitants and to demand protection money from them; and possibly some people used the general disorder to settle their private quarrels. For example, John Bokeden, one time servant of another tenant at Woodditton, broke into the close and house of Sir Henry English, the sheriff of Cambridgeshire, who lived at Woodditton, and took goods and chattels valued at 40s. A brass (somewhat mutilated) to Sir Henry and his wife Margaret may still be seen in Woodditton church (see the illustration below).

SIR HENRY ENGLISH AND MARGARET HIS WIFE.

**Illustration 6**
**The brass to Sir Henry English and his wife in Woodditton church, 1393**

23

I have mentioned the names of the leaders in New-market's surrounding villages to suggest that, although Newmarket people do not seem to have taken any active part in the revolt, the disturbances in the neighbourhood cannot but have had their effect on Newmarket itself. Two incidents affecting the town are in fact recorded and confirm this. Simon the vicar of Mildenhall was arrested by the sheriff because he 'with many other malefactors' on Friday 14 June came 'in warlike manner arrayed' to the house of Ralph atte Wyke, one of the King's officials, in Newmarket. He threatened to behead Ralph and burn down his house if he did not deliver up to him at Mildenhall Ralph of Swaffham's daughter, alleged by Simon to have been abducted by Ralph atte Wyke. Ralph paid him protection money, but the whole incident caused 'manifest affright and disturbance to the whole town.'[30] There is still today a Wyck Hall Stud on the Dullingham road just outside Newmarket; perhaps this was where Ralph atte Wyke lived in 1381.

On the following day, Saturday 15 June, as recorded at a court held in Newmarket on 3 July, the presenting jurors reported that one 'William Sharp, a taverner, came with force and arms to Newmarket and entered John of Icklingham's close there, breaking the king's peace.' He threatened John's wife, Katherine, and extorted from her the sum of four marks (£2 13s 4d, a considerable sum in those days).[31] We know where John of Icklingham lived; his holding was on the Cambridgeshire side of the High Street, abutting to the west on 'Dundich' (presumably the water course where it runs today through the Jockey Club grounds), with its southern boundary on the Icknield Way — the Icknield Way then ran not down the High Street but straight through what we now know as Palace Street besides All Saints' Church to the present Queensberry Road (see plan D on pages 32–33).

By 20 June the revolt was petering out, and the leader in Norfolk; one Geoffrey Litster, decided to send an embassy to London to ask for a general pardon. Two knights and three peasants, with a large sum of money, started on their way, but were intercepted at Icklingham by the Bishop of Norwich, Henry le Spencer, who had already crushed the rising in Huntingdon and Cambridge. The two knights were spared, but the three peasants were immediately executed and their heads fixed on poles in Newmarket as a warning to other rebels. No doubt Newmarket was chosen because it was the market centre for the villages from which the local rebel leaders already mentioned came.

Newmarket has however a more permanent memorial to the Peasants' Revolt. In St Mary's Church there has been since early in the 15th century a chapel or aisle dedicated to St Tebold.[32] St Tebold has now been identified with Simon Theobald of Sudbury who was Archbishop of Canterbury from 1375 to 1381 and Lord Chancellor from 1380 to 1381. He was regarded by the rebel leaders in London as responsible for many of their injustices, and was executed as a scapegoat by the mob on Tower Hill on 14 June 1381.[33] His murder caused him to be recognized as a martyr and in some quarters he was compared with St Thomas à Becket (the south aisle in St Mary's Church is dedicated to St Thomas). It has been suggested that St Mary's was extended at the end of the 14th or the beginning of the 15th century, and that the extension was dedicated to St Tebold as a near contemporary and local martyr.

If we ask why Newmarket was at the receiving end and not the spearpoint of the revolt, the answer probably lies in its very nature as a new town. The revolt seems to have been caused by an accumulation of injustices. Villeins living on manors were feeling more and more oppressed by the terms under which they lived and worked. They resented very strongly the imposition of three poll taxes in 1377–1380 and the enforcement of the Statute of Labourers in 1351 which had restricted wage rates to pre-Black Death levels. The inhabitants of Newmarket were, as we have seen, for the most part free men and did not live under the old manorial restrictions; the Statute of Labourers would perhaps have affected them little. Nor were they under the grasping control of ecclesiastical bodies like the abbey at Bury St Edmunds. On the whole it might have been to their interest to remain neutral and not to get too involved.

## Chapter Four

## THE ECONOMY OF THE NEW TOWN

It is sometimes said that Newmarket was a small village before King James I discovered it and it became 'royal' Newmarket. If by village we mean a community whose economy was agriculturally based, then Newmarket never was a village. As we have seen, it began its life as a community based round its market, and it has continued that way, as a small market town to this day, although its economy since the 17th century has been based increasingly on the stable and the stud, and to some extent on the caravan.

One way of looking at Newmarket's economy in the early days is to compare it with that of Ditton Valens, one of the Woodditton manors (the other was Ditton Camoys) which had links with Newmarket similar to those of Exning. We can do this by tabulating the income and expenditure of the two manors. Fortunately we have more or less contemporary account rolls of both, of Newmarket for 1403–1404 and of Ditton Valens for 1394–1395.[1]

The table below compares the incomes of the two manors. It is obvious that the income (and expenditure) for the manor of Ditton Valens could be paralleled from countless similar agriculturally based manors throughout England. Even a town like Mildenhall has similar items on the income side of its accounts for the year 1411–1412.[2] Newmarket in this respect then is atypical. Common to both Newmarket and Ditton Valens are fixed rents, land 'farmed out' and court fines; such items are common to the account rolls of most manors. Second the sources of income are markedly different in the two manors. Newmarket's economy is clearly centred on its market and fair; Ditton Valens' is equally clearly centred on wholly agricultural items, grain from its arable fields, timber from its woods, and wool and milk from its sheep and cows. Surprising to us today is that the income from Ditton Valens is over three times that from Newmarket.

| | Newmarket | | | Ditton Valens | | |
|---|---|---|---|---|---|---|
| Fixed rents | £2 | 3s | 1d | £2 | 8s | 6d |
| Land 'farmed out' | £2 | 3s | 8d | £8 | 5s | 4d |
| Court fines | £2 | 4s | 0½d | £1 | 17s | 6d |
| Market tolls | | 18s | 0d | | nil | |
| Rent of market stalls | £1 | 16s | 10d | | nil | |
| Profits of fair | £3 | 6s | 8d | | nil | |
| Mill 'farmed out' | | nil | | £1 | 10s | 0d |
| Sale of stock | | nil | | £3 | 11s | 10d |
| Sale of wool | | nil | | £8 | 16s | 6d |
| Sale of timber | | nil | | £5 | 6s | 6d |
| Sale of dairy produce | | nil | | £9 | 0s | 0d |
| Sale of corn | | nil | | £6 | 6s | 8d |
| Arrears from previous year | | 17s | 3d | | nil | |
| Total | £13 | 9s | 6½d | £47 | 2s | 10d |

Now let us look at the expenditure of the two manors. These are so completely different that there is no advantage in tabulating them in parallel.

**Newmarket 1403–1404**

| | | | |
|---|---|---|---|
| Tithes payable to the chaplain of St Mary's Church from fair | | 6s | 8d |
| Expenses etc of the steward of the manor | £1 | 2s | 6d |
| Sundry small expenses | £2 | 4s | 1d |
| Balance due to the lord of the manor | £9 | 16s | 3½d |
| | | | |
| Total | £13 | 9s | 6½d |

The sundry small expenses include 1s 4d for medicine for one of the horses of the lord of the manor, and 3s 4d in payment of a subsidy to King Henry VI.

**Ditton Valens 1394–1395**

| | | | |
|---|---|---|---|
| Maintenance of ploughs, carts, mill etc | £1 | 3s | 8d |
| Purchases of grain and stock | £1 | 9s | 0d |
| Expenses of sheepfold | | 2s | 6d |
| Expenses of ploughing, harrowing etc | £2 | 8s | 5d |
| Expenses of harvesting | £7 | 10s | 6d |
| Wages | £3 | 13s | 4d |
| Lord's sundry expenses | £1 | 13s | 0d |
| Out payments ('forensic' expenses) | £1 | 11s | 8d |
| Sundry small expenses | £3 | 5s | 10d |
| Sundry 'allowances' | £1 | 17s | 6½d |
| Balance due to the lord of the manor | £22 | 7s | 4½d |
| | | | |
| Total | £47 | 2s | 10d |

In medieval accounts the income was always the estimated income, not the realised income, and so generally on the expenditure side were 'allowances', that is income that had not been realised perhaps because a tenant had left the manor, perhaps because a fine imposed by the courts had not been paid. Out payments (called 'forensic' expenses) referred to items strictly outside the manor, for example, as we shall see later in this chapter, fish for the Alingtons' household at Horseheath.

We shall notice several things about these accounts. First the lord of the manor of Newmarket gets a much better return proportionate to his expenditure than that of Ditton Valens, £9 16s 3½d out of £13 9s 6½d compared with £22 7s 4½d out of £47 2s 10d. Secondly the reason for this is clear. The expenses of the agriculturally based manor of Ditton Valens are much higher than those of the market and fair based manor of Newmarket. Thirdly although much of the labour on the Ditton Valens manor was done by the eighteen villeins living on the manor, the wages bill shows that the lord of the manor had to employ a carter, two ploughmen, a drover, a shepherd and a cowman, as well as occasional labour; he also had a bailiff or agent. The only people to whom the lord of the manor of Newmarket paid wages were his steward and his bailiff; his steward's main responsibilities seem to have been to preside over the manorial courts, while his bailiff was primarily a collector of rents.

Another item in these accounts shows how little Newmarket was agriculturally based. The reverse side of account rolls in medieval times normally contained a list of manorial assets in the form of farm stock and grain. Although this list is missing from the Ditton Valens account rolls for 1394–1395, an earlier account roll for the manor records the amount of wheat, rye, oats and barley and the number of horses, cows, sheep, pigs, hens and capons belonging to the lord of the manor — in 1300 manorial stock included six cows (two with calf), three pigs, a cock and four hens![3] Newmarket account rolls for the 15th century have either no entry at all or the following:

**Wheat**
No wheat issuing from the lord's lands this year because none was sown in the previous year (the same entry goes for rye, peas, barley, oats and malt).

**Carthorses**
No carthorses in the lord's lands this year because none came into it, either stray or native (the same entry goes for all other farm stock except capons, i.e. castrated cocks; five of the tenants paid part of their rent in capons, generally at Christmas — by 1472 this had been commuted into cash).[4]

Now of course these entries do not mean that no crops were grown and no animals were about in the field of Newmarket. Several tenants rented arable land from the lord of the manor, for example in 1472 Arthur Greysson had six acres of land at the Chalkpits by Black Bear Lane.[5] Entries in the earlier court rolls include fines for trespass in the lord's meadow by the cows, horses or pigs of his tenants. What these entries do mean is that so far as the lord of the manor was concerned, he 'farmed out' all his arable land and maintained no farm stock of his own; indeed he sold all the hay in his meadow and actually had to buy wheat etc in his own market.

We have established that Newmarket was always market based and not agriculturally based. The implications of this are important for our understanding of 15th century life in Newmarket. Firstly a weekly market and a fair twice a year meant that traders, merchants and others were always coming and going in and out of Newmarket; it is probably true to say that there has never been a time when Newmarket-born people outnumbered those born elsewhere. Life in an agriculturally based manor like Ditton Valens was quite different; until villages in comparatively recent times provided holiday homes and houses for the retired and the commuter, 'foreigners' were few and far between and were hardly welcomed. We shall see in a later chapter from how far afield people came to Newmarket for various reasons.

Secondly a manor like Ditton Valens was a very integrated unit, with the inhabitants dependent on the lord of the manor and interdependent on each other. A glance for example at the plan of Laxton in Nottinghamshire, one of the few villages still operating on the medieval system, will show how inter-related all agricultural activities were.[6] The feudal system that created and maintained these agricultural activities never really operated in Newmarket, partly because Newmarket was a new development and partly because many of those who lived and worked in Newmarket had their roots elsewhere. Perhaps the complaint that there is little community spirit in Newmarket goes back to its origins and its market based economy.

We are fortunate to have extant in the Suffolk Record

Office at Bury St Edmunds two series of account rolls for the manor of Newmarket in the 15th century, one for the years 1428–1440 (with one or two omissions) and the other for the years 1472–1483.[7] These account rolls give us an interesting insight into the economy of the manor, and thereby tell us something about the life of the town itself. We have already noticed that the profits of our Newmarket manor in 1403–1404 were proportionately larger than those for the agriculturally based manor of Ditton Valens. The two series of accounts just mentioned show how small were the expenses of the Argenteins and Alingtons and how much they were able to take out of the manor.

| Years | Average Income | Average Expenditure | Profit |
|---|---|---|---|
| 1428–1440 | £21 0s 0d | £2 0s 0d | £19 0s 0d |
| 1472–1483 | £17 10s 0d | £5 0s 0d | £12 10s 0d |

By the standards of 1981 these sums of course sound like peanuts! But in fact we probably have to use a multiplier of several hundreds to get their present day values.[8]

The decrease in income and the increase of expenditure between 1428–1440 and 1472–1483 are of interest because they reflect changes in the social and economic life of Newmarket. First look at the decrease in income. There are two areas in which this is marked. First the annual average income from the fair held round St Simon and St Jude's Day (28 October) has gone down from £2 6s 0d to 18s. In the 1428–1440 series of accounts a regular item of expenditure runs as follows:

To hire of six men to collect moneys from the profits and proceeds of the fair 2s; to purchase of purses for the same 3d.

Both items are missing from the later series of accounts. If we ask where the Newmarket fair was held, the answer almost certainly is St Mary's Square, called Fairstead in the Enclosure Award map of 1821. We in Newmarket today associate fairs with the Severals, with Fairstead House on its fringe, but in the 15th century Severals was in one of the Exning manors and not in the manor of Newmarket, and the Argenteins and the Alingtons would not have been able to pocket the proceeds of a fair held

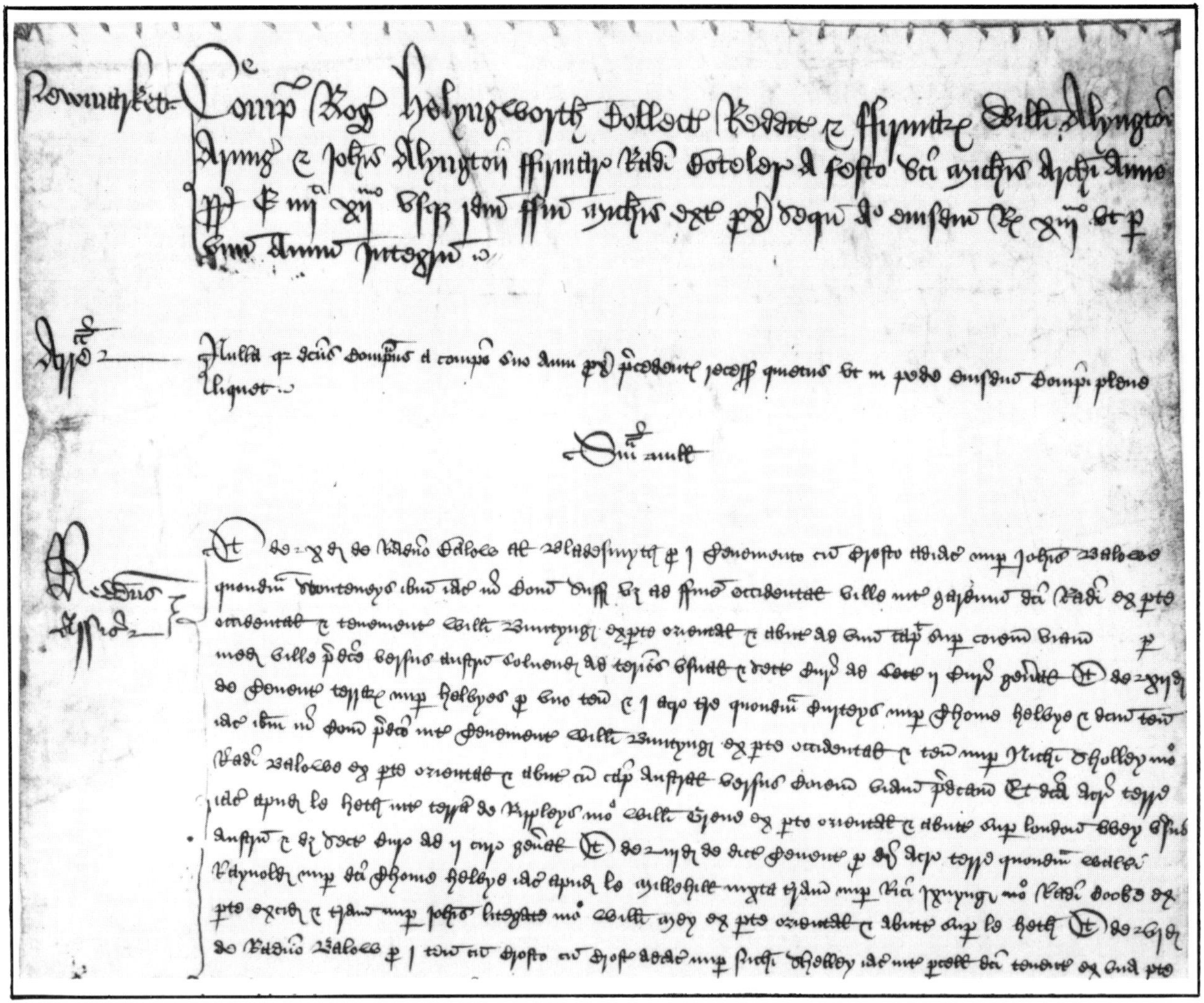

**Illustration 7**

The beginning of the account roll for the manor of Newmarket for 1472/3, from which much of our information about 15th century Newmarket has been drawn.

The opening four lines may be translated thus:

> Newmarkett  The account of Roger Holyngworth Collector of Rents and Payments for William Alyngton Esquire and for John Alyngton, 'Farmer' for Ralph Boteler, for the whole year from St Michael's Day in the 12th year of the reign of King Edward IV until the same day in the 13th year of the same King.

The first entry, after 'arrears' from the previous year, records the payment of 10d as fixed rent due from Ralph Balow *alias* Bladesmyth for a holding with craft lying at the western end of the town (see plan D on pages 32–33).

28

outside their own manor. We can picture the six hired men going round with their purses and collecting the fair tolls from the stalls and at the lanes leading into St Mary's Square. Another feature of the 1428–1440 accounts is that they all record the payment of tithe (varying from 4s to 6s 8d) on the profits of the fair 'to the chaplain of the chantry chapel of St Mary, built for the health of the souls of the lords of the manor'; this item too is missing from the later series of accounts. Tithes would normally be paid to the parish church, in the case of Newmarket, to St Martin's, Exning, but presumably there was some arrangement by which the tithes in connection with the fair were paid to St Mary's, perhaps because the fair was held in St Mary's Square. At all events it is clear that between 1440 and 1472 the popularity and profitability of Newmarket fair had waned, possibly because Stourbridge Fair at Cambridge had become not only inter-regional but even international in character.

The other area in which income declined between 1428–1440 and 1472–1483 was in court fines; the annual average during the first period was about £5, and in the second £1 15s 0d. In the 15th century the lord of the manor could take the fines imposed in four different courts held in his manor. There was first of all the Leet, or View of Frankpledge, held once a year on 1 August, concerned with offences against the realm, in particular the king's peace. There was second the General Court or Court Baron as it was later called; this was held twice a year, at Easter and All Saints' tide (1 November) and was concerned with offences against the manor. All inhabitants of Newmarket were expected to attend the Leet, and all manorial tenants owed 'suit of court' at the General Court. The Fair Court was held twice a year, round St Barnabas' Day (11 June) and St Simon and St Jude's Day (28 October), when the two fairs were held; it was concerned primarily with repairs to stalls and shops and seems to have been almost the annual general meeting of the Market Court. This was held in theory every week but in practice every two or three weeks, always on a Tuesday, market day then and now, and, as we shall see in a later chapter, was concerned

primarily with the recovery of debts. In the 15th century all four courts functioned and brought in a considerable sum to the lord of the manor. By the end of the century their power had clearly declined, and by the end of the 16th century only the View of Frankpledge and the General Court had survived.

Rent from land 'farmed out' remained more or less constant at £2 a year during the whole of the 15th century. When we remember that our Newmarket at this time consisted only of the old wards of St Mary's and All Saints', we shall realize that the amount of land available for letting out to farm was limited. Presumably the limit had already been reached in 1428, and so there could be no increase in this item.

The one area in which a higher annual income is recorded for the later period of 1472–1483 is in the rent of stalls and shops in the market place. This averaged £4 4s 0d in 1428–1440 and £6 15s 0d in 1472–1483. This seems to have been partly due to an increase in the number of stalls and shops; there were no less than 108 in 1472. The rent from these was not the only source of revenue from traders for the lord of the manor; he could exact tolls from various items sold in the market. New tenants had to pay an entry fee (called a fine) on taking over the tenancy; naturally there were new tenants who tried to evade this fee by quietly taking over a stall or shop, and were duly fined when caught at the appropriate manorial court.

Another reason for the increase in income from stalls and shops may have been more efficient administration by the bailiff of the manor. No rent was received from ten stalls and shops for some years in the period 1428–1440 because of a defect in the water supply or possibly drains. Expenditure on the market place had also increased. The only building on the whole of his Newmarket manor for which the lord was responsible was the Tollbooth, in the centre of the market place and the hub round which the market revolved. It seems to have been a two-storied stone building, with an upper storey which was let out. It had to be kept in good repair and under lock and key, no doubt because it was here that dues and fines were paid and the standard measures for the town were kept.

A major repair seems to have been undertaken in 1472–1473 as the following items show:

10s paid to John Stedman, carpenter, for the repair of the Tollbooth, inclusive, under agreement;
5s paid for 195 iron nails bought for the same;
4s paid for eight pairs of 'hynges' and 'hokes';
8d for putting the said 'hokes' into the stone walls;
2d for binding the 'splentes';
9s for meals for the carpenter and his workmen;
12d for three cartloads of clay;
2s for plastering the 'mydilwal' inside the Tollbooth;
3s 8d for one load of burnt lime;
6d for three cartloads of sand;
4s for filling and 'pargetyng' of the walls there;
8d for one lock with key for the door of the Tollbooth.

Perhaps £2 does not sound very much for the work done, but it may represent the expenditure of £800 to £1000 today.

It will have been clear that the Argenteins and the Alingtons as lords of the manor of Newmarket took more out of it than they put in, regarding it as a source of income rather than a responsibility. The Alingtons, as we have seen, had their main seat at Horseheath. None the less they, or rather their bailiff for them, did some of their shopping occasionally in Newmarket. Accounts for the 1470s show that they bought in Newmarket rye, pork and peas, and surprisingly fish, and sea fish at that.

For example their accounts for 1479–1480 included 3s 4d for fish bought from John Osteller of Newmarket and 3s 4d for 'porpoz' bought from the same. In the previous year they had spent 18d for one cade (cask) of 'spyrlyng' (smelt), 3s 4d for rabbits in connection with Elizabeth Alington's wedding, 26s 8d for two barrels of white herrings (i.e. herrings salted but not smoked), 21s for three cades of red herrings (i.e. herrings cured by smoking) and 3s for two cades of 'le sprottes' (sprats). The accounts for 1475–1476 included a sum of 20s 2d for 200 herrings, whelks and turbot in red wine. As traders were frequently fined in the manorial courts at the beginning of the 15th century for selling fish (on two occasions oysters) at an excessive price, evidently the fish stall in the market must have been a regular feature. Perhaps this is not so surprising when we remember that until a few years ago there was a rather dilapidated 'kipper house' behind the 18th century weatherboard houses in Market Street, and that Reach, only a few miles away, was a medieval inland port that carried on trade until the 19th century.

Unfortunately no account rolls for the manor survive beyond the end of the 15th century. Sixteenth century court rolls record fines for various offences and the transfer of shops and stalls in the market and of property in the High Street. Throughout our period the economy of Newmarket centred round the market and property rented out in the High Street.

## Chapter Five

# THE FIFTEENTH CENTURY: THE HIGH STREET

For our history of Newmarket in the 13th and 14th centuries we have had to draw largely from documentary material which looks at our town from the outside, enquiries requested or charters granted by the Crown, or items extracted from records basically concerned with a wider world. When we come to the 15th century, our material is much more local.[1] In this and the following chapter we shall try to draw a picture of our 15th century forefathers as we can discover it from these contemporary documents. For convenience it is simplest to divide the people who used Newmarket into two groups, those who actually lived in the town, for the most part down either side of the High Street, and those who traded in it week by week in the market, and twice a year at the two fairs.

## Holdings

Most of the inhabitants of our town lived in holdings (the latin word is *tenementa*) on either side of the High Street. A very detailed account roll for 1472/73 shows that there were at least twenty-six holdings on the Exning side of the High Street, of which all but four were on the rent roll of the Newmarket manor; and there were a further nineteen on the Woodditton side, of which as we might expect only ten were held from the manor of Newmarket — the other nine were probably in the manor of Ditton Valens.[2]

'Holding' is a vague word, but in our Newmarket context it always seems to signify an enclosed area of an acre or under, with a house or messuage in which the tenant lived. In it he could grow a simple crop and keep a pig, a horse, a cow, perhaps a sheep, and a chicken or two; as enclosed it could be called a close or later a homeclose. The holdings between our present Black Bear Lane and Church Lane reached back to what is now Fitzroy Street; this was then only a lane by which the tenants could get to their strips of land in the great common field beyond (see plan D on pages 32–33). The re-siting of the market place in the Rookery area sometime in the 14th century makes it difficult to judge the original size of the holdings which lay between what is now Wellington Street (then Market Lane) and the Clock Tower; they probably went back more or less to Fred Archer Way, linking Wellington Street with Fordham Road. The opening up of the Rookery car park gives us something of an idea of how the holdings ran. As for the ten holdings between Black Bear Lane and Church Lane, we have only to walk round the block enclosed by Fitzroy Street and the High Street to see their old boundary lines (see plan D mentioned above). On the other side of the High Street the sites of the original holdings are much more difficult to determine because in the 17th century the whole area from the Rutland Arms down to Sun Lane was pulled down to build the Royal Palace and its complex. We have already noticed that the Icknield Way did not run down the High Street, but down Palace Street past All Saints' Church. The holdings on the Woodditton side of the High Street lay between the Icknield Way to the south east and the High Street to the north west.

The manorial tenants who lived on either side of the High Street all paid rent twice a year, at Easter and Michaelmas; although the amount varied from tenant to tenant, the actual rent was fixed in the sense that it was fixed for the life of the manor and was never changed for any individual holding. In times of inflation this benefited the tenant but the lord of the manor could and did increase the amount of entry fee due from a new tenant. The tenant held his holding to himself; if he wanted to dispose of it, he had to surrender it to the lord of the manor. Sometimes he would share the tenancy with friends or relatives, called co-feoffees, and would ask them in his will to make a lawful transfer to his widow.

This was what William Baron did in 1439; he left his house in Newmarket called the Griffin and lands in Ditton Valens, Saxton and Cheveley to his wife, requesting his co-feoffees to see that she had them. Our 15th century testators generally left their holdings to their wives, 'for the term of her life'; on her death they were usually sold and the proceeds divided between the children and disposed of 'for the good of my soul' in charity. These tenancies, with their fixed rents, possibly go back to the beginning of the 13th century, with a few additions during the next century.

## Plan D — Key

*The names in italics are those of the tenants in the account roll of 1472/3; all others are of those mentioned in this book.*

*\*denotes a resident not on the rent roll of the manor of Newmarket.*

  1. John Balow (*alias* Bladesmith), *Ralph Balow*
\* 2. *William Buntyng*
  3. *Thomas Helbye*
  4. *Ralph Balow*
  5. *John Wykes*
\* 6. THE SHIP: *William Nameskyll*
  7. THE BEAR: *Thomas Depden*
  8. John Pere, Richard Gateward, *John Laste*
  9. *William Aylenoth*
10. William Palgrave, *John Cracke*
11. John Ray, Ralph Hancocks, *Thomas Percyvale*
\*12. John Ray, *Ralph Lote*
13. Ralph Gateward, Richard Gateward, *Ralph Lote*
14. John Leiston, *Roger Holyngworth*
15. *Henry Dale*, THE MAIDENHEAD: John Archer
16. *William Mey*, Christopher Roughe
17. THE SWORD: John Higham, *Arthur Greysson,*
    John Ayers, David Ayers
18. THE POUND: John Higham, Richard Gateward,
    *John Bonde*
\*19. THE CHRISTOPHER: *John Wright*
20. THE BELL: Henry Dale
21. John Upryght, *John Yeresley*
22. John Upryght, *John Yeresley*
23. *Thomas Depden*
24. *Katherine Poperyk*

32

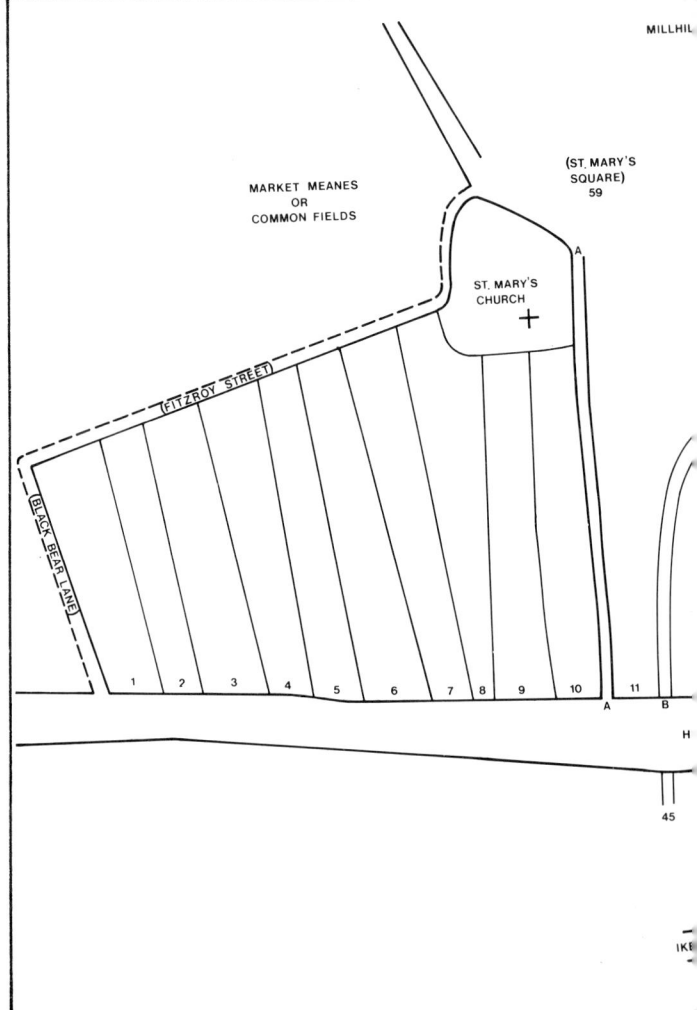

**Plan D**
**NEWMARKET as it may have been in 1472**
*(modern names in brackets)*

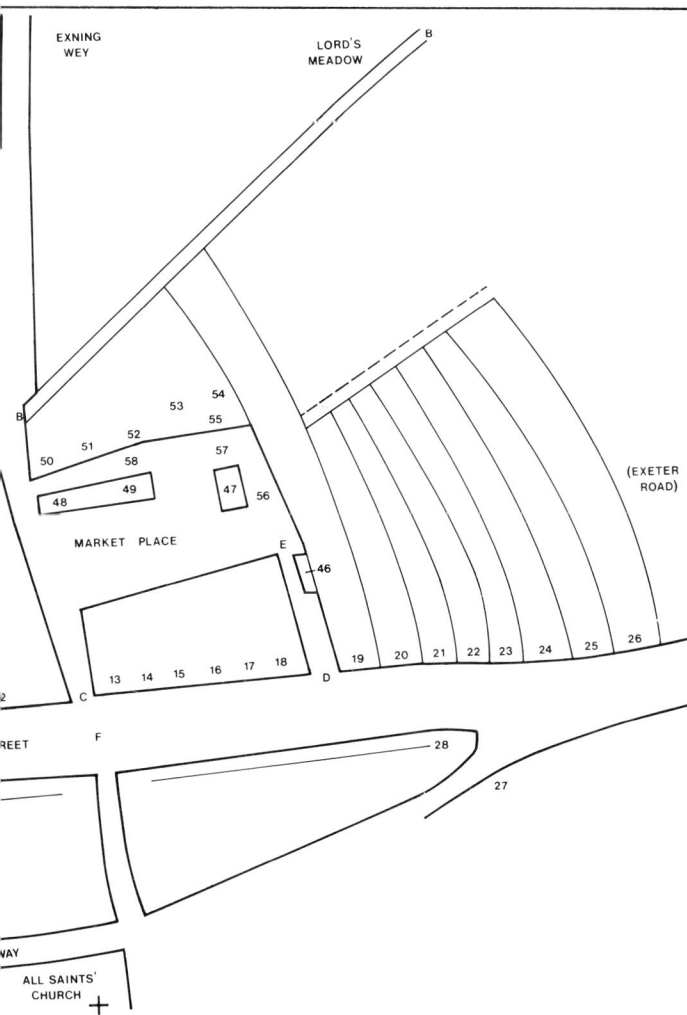

25. *John Wykes*
*26. *John Bede*
27. *Thomas Pateryk*
*28. THE RAM: John Withall
29. THE HART: John Redere, *the Prior of Fordham*
30. Walter Bocher, *Henry Cheveley*
31. William Cheveley, Thomas Cheveley, *Henry Cheveley*
32. Nicholas Bocher, *William Jourdon*
*33. *Henry Cheveley*
*34. *John Leycestre*
35. *Ralph Cooke*
*36. *Roger Holyngworth*
*37. *Richard Deresley*
38. THE SWAN: John Kyrkeby, *Roger Holyngworth*
*39. THE GRIFFIN: William Baron, *Arthur Greysson,* Leonard Beale, Richard Hamerton
40. THE BULL: Richard Motte, *Arthur Greysson*
*41. *Ralph Lote*
42. THE SARACEN'S HEAD: William Farwell, Roger Mayner, *Arthur Greysson*
*43. The Vicar of Wickhambrook, *Thomas Depden*
44. John Ickelyngham, *John Wykes*
*45. Dundich
46. BULLSYARD: *John Wykes*
47. Thomas Quylter, *Ellis Jordon*
48. *John Kydde*
49. *Ralph Lote*
50. Ralph Lote, *Roger Holyngworth and John Cracke*
51. THE FANFAIR: *Simon Funston*
52. Ralph Lote, *John Kervin*
53. Ralph Lote, *John Grygge*
54. Ralph Lote, *Henry Dale*
55. THE FANFAIR WAY: Ralph Lote, *John Glover*
56. BULLSYARD
57. THE FAIR WAY
58. THE SHRAGGERY ROW
59. FAIRSTEAD or ST MARY'S SQUARE

A. Church Lane
B. The Water-course
C. Market Lane (now Wellington Street)
D. The road to the Cornhill (now Market Street)
E. The Cornhill
F. The Cross

There was also a second group of tenants, who, although living within the manor, owed little or no obligation to its lord, except to attend the Leet or View of Frankpledge once a year and pay a nominal fee when a new heir succeeded to the holding. Many of those marked with an asterisk on plan D on pages 32–33 (for example William Buntyng and John Wright at the Christopher) were almost certainly such tenants. The manorial records are not interested in them since they are not a source of income to the lord of the manor.

By the end of the 15th century there was a third type of tenant in Newmarket. By then there was a group of some half a dozen houses lying round the market place (where the Rookery now is). These were let for a period of years, and in time of inflation the lord could increase the rent. The location of all these holdings round the market place and only there helps to confirm that the development round the re-sited market is later than that in the High Street.

## People

Twenty wills of the people who lived in the High Street in the 15th century have survived; although of course they represent only a small portion of all the inhabitants of Newmarket, and at that only those with sufficient property and goods to make wills, none the less they give us some kind of picture of our 15th century forebears.

First they were people of the late middle ages, and their wills reflect the attitudes of their time. They were in a formal sense religious people, concerned very much that after death they should not suffer the pains of hell. Every will begins with the formal commendation of the soul to God Almighty, the blessed Virgin Mary and all the saints of heaven. By a normal formality of the time bequests were invariably made to 'the high altar' of either St Mary's Church or All Saints' Church, 'for my tithes forgotten or underpaid'; the sum given varies according to the wealth of the testator, from 6d to £1. Several testators stipulate a (standard) bequest of 8 marks (£5 6s 8d) to a suitable priest 'to celebrate [say mass] for my soul and for the souls of my parents and my

benefactors departed'. Some bequeath a sum for a 'trental', that is the saying of thirty masses for the repose of their souls. This is all very standard medieval practice; 'my soul's health' was very much a medieval concern.

Some testators however go much beyond this, perhaps because their religion was more than formal, or perhaps (more likely) because they could afford it. William Palgrave, for example, dying in 1451, bequeathed to every chaplain present at his funeral 4d, to every clerk 2d, and to every poor man 1d; similarly William Baron whom we have already mentioned. Again this was standard medieval practice for those who could afford it, to ensure the maximum number of people to say prayers for one's soul. Sums of money are left for general church objects, such as for 'the reparation' (presumably the fabric) of St Mary's or All Saints' churches, and sometimes for that of churches in the neighbourhood. John Bonde, for example, in 1476 left 6s 8d each to Snailwell, Fordham and Soham churches, presumably churches with which he had some special ties; and Simon Funston, in 1497, left a coomb (four bushels) of malt each to 'the Chyrche werkes' of Cheveley, Ditton and All Saints', Newmarket. Bequests are made for more specific church objects, such as William Baron's 66s 8d for the making of the roodloft in St Mary's, Thomas Quylter's 4s for 'the reparation' of the bell of the same church, John Ray's hive of bees to supply wax for the candles before the statue of the blessed Virgin Mary in All Saints' Church, Adam Colakyr's cauldron to 'heat the lights' (melt the beeswax?) in the Easter Tomb at the same church, William Folkys' 20s to St Mary's Church 'to the stolling [seating] or Rode lofting which that they beginn first', and John Grygge's 3s 4d 'to the reparation of the Ile [aisle] of seynt Tebold' in the same church. Bequests are also made to one or all of the four orders of friars and to religious guilds. The latter were not the same as trade guilds such as the Haberdashers' Guild. Their objects were both religious and social. They supplied perhaps a light before the image of the saint after whom they were named, sometimes maintained a side chapel in the parish church or even supported a parish priest. Socially they were rather like a club, supporting each other, even building guild-halls (as at Kentford) for church ales and the like. St Mary's had a Guild of St Thomas to which Adam Colakyr left the value of half a brass pot when sold; as St Mary's has even today a chapel of St Thomas, no doubt this was the responsibility of the guild.

More altruistic perhaps (or was he a shrewd business-man?) were John Ray's bequests of 6s 8d for the repair of the lane called Saxton Lane leading to Kirtling, and of the lane called Dermundeslane leading to Ditton Park, an indication that local roads had to be maintained by private enterprise and manorial oversight.

What did they do for a living? Only two of our twenty testators expressly state their occupations. John Upryght describes himself as 'guardian of the old chapel of blessed Mary of Newmarket in the parish of Exning'; he was in fact the parish priest in St Mary's for over thirty years, from 1412 until his death in 1445. St Mary's was still only a chapel of ease in the parish of St Martin's, Exning, its mother church, and John Upryght recognizes this in his will by bequeathing 6s 8d to the high altar of Exning, 12d to the parish priest there and 6d to Thomas Bladsmyth its holy water clerk. His pocket breviary he left to Master Nicholas Leycestre who in fact succeeded him as parish priest at St Mary's. But as he left £5 to the 'reparation' of the chapel of St Mary, his true love was there. If we ask, why the *old* chapel of blessed Mary, the answer seems to be that soon after St Mary's was built, round about 1380, another chapel, called the new chapel of blessed Mary, was built in the same 'vill', under the patronage of the Prior of Thetford, and annexed to the parish church of Woodditton.[3] This eventually became All Saints' Church, and remained 'annexed' to the parish of Woodditton as a chapel of ease until it became a parish in its own right in 1868.

No doubt John Upryght lived in St Mary's parsonage on the west side of the church. He also had two holdings on the north side of the High Street (see plan D) and had pieces of glebe to cultivate. *The Glebe Terrier* of 1633 records that the parson of St Mary's had forty-three pieces of land scattered over the fields of Exning, Wood-ditton and Newmarket, varying from two acres to one rood in size, some thirty acres in all.[4] We do not know whether John Upryght had the same amount of glebe in the 15th century, but however much he had John will have been kept fairly busy, looking after his hold-ings and his strips in the fields as well as his parishioners.

The only other person in the wills who describes himself is John Grygge whose occupation is given as a husbandman, that is a farmer. The account roll of 1472 (he died in 1488) shows that he had two holdings, both at the back of the market place, apparently backing on to the water-course (see plan D on pages 32–33). He also had a shop in the market, probably attached to his house. His will shows however that this was a side-line:

I wyll that all my Shepe be sold by myne wyffe and the mony of the Sale of the seid Shepe comyng be disposed after the discrecion of her. Also I bequeth to the seid Felice [Phyllis] myn wyffe & Robert Larkyng her sone [by her first husband] alle myn hors with the carte harneys and alle othre thynges longyng to the same . . . Also I wyll that Robert Lorkyn myn sone [strictly stepson] have on of the beste of myn hors at his owne schoys.

Evidently Phyllis did not sell the 'shepe' because when she died in 1496 she willed that Robert and his sister Joan 'part [share]' them. No doubt John Grygge's sheep were pastured in his 'londes lying in the Townes of Ixning and Dytton'. His bequests for the 'reparation' of the churches of Woodditton and Stetchworth and to the highway in Saxton between Dernell Lane and a 'grene therby lyng' suggest that he was one of the many folk who through the centuries have made their way from the neighbouring villages, hoping to make their fortune in Newmarket itself. Perhaps it was his father, another John Grygge, who was one of the jurors at a general court of Ditton Valens manor in 1406.

Of the other eighteen 15th century wills three specifi-cally mention inns or alehouses, suggesting that the three people concerned were occupied in supplying refresh-ments and accommodation to travellers or to those coming to the market on market days. Arthur Greysson was certainly the wealthiest of these, for he left to his wife Margery (a very common Newmarket name), when he died in 1489, the Griffin, the Sword, the Bull and the Saracen's Head (see plan D on pages 32–33). The two latter he had only just bought and instructed his wife to pay the £92 still due to the vendors, Roger Mayner and Richard Motte of Dalham. It sounds as if he may have been something of a tycoon, speculating in property. He also had land in Woodditton and was in fact steward of the lord of the manor there in the 1460s.

The account roll of 1472/73 to which we have frequently referred records that at the end of the 15th century there were at least twelve inns or alehouses down the High Street; on the north side the Ship, the Bear, the Sword, the Christopher and the Bell, and on the south side the Hart, the Swan, the Ram, the Griffin, the Bull, the Saracen's Head and the Angel (see plan D). The Christopher is of particular interest. There is only one royal visit to Newmarket recorded before King James I, and that is of Queen Margaret of Anjou, the wife of King Henry VI. During her stay in the town in 1452/53, a stable belonging to Richard Salisbury of Soham, rented by one John Wright, was burnt down and John Wright's beds, corn and household stuff were destroyed. Queen Margaret gave Richard £10 and John Wright £6 6s 8d by way of compensation. As John Wright is named in the 1472 account roll as the tenant of the Christopher, we may perhaps assume that this was where the fire of 1452/53 occurred and occasioned Queen Margaret's gift.[5] There was also an alehouse north of the market place, the Fanfair.

That the provision of refreshments for travellers and others was a major occupation of Newmarket folk in the 15th century is confirmed by the evidence of the General Court Rolls for 1399–1413. The chief offences presented to this court were concerned with breaches of what were called the assize of bread and ale. Sometime in the middle of the 13th century it was laid down as a national ordinance that the price and quality of bread and ale should be determined by the market price of wheat and barley.[6] Every year the court appointed inspectors of bread and ale, to see that the assize was kept and to report on breaches. Offenders were fined and the money accruing went to the lord of the manor.

Illustration 8        A fifteenth century alewife at work

In some courts *all* alewives – the brewers of ale were generally women – were fined as a matter of course for breaking the assize of ale; this may well have been a form of licensing. At Mildenhall for example in 1299 no less than forty-four men and women were so fined.[7] This does not seem to have been the custom in Newmarket, because the fines vary in amount and there are occasional omissions each year. Over the period of twelve years (1400–1412) for which we have the general court rolls, there was an average of seventeen offending alewives at each court held, and a total of sixty different alewives in all. And more than that, an average of ten *other* women in each court, another fifty in all, were fined during this period as 'regraters' of ale, that is they bought ale to sell retail at above the stipulated price. In other words there were in this period over 110 women engaged in the brewing and selling of ale! All these women were required to sell their ale by pots certified to hold a pint and to produce their measured pint pots to the general court every half year. From the numbers fined for not producing their pots, they clearly felt it more profitable to pay the fine than to have their pots condemned as being undersized!

Evidently it was a bye-law in Newmarket that in the selling of ale residents should be given preference over travellers, but it was clearly more profitable then as now to sell to 'foreigners', as the following entry in one of the rolls suggests:

> John Redere's wife is a communal alewife and had 36 gallons of ale and would not sell to John Wykes, Walter Bocher, Thomas Pere, Thomas Sowtere and others, but kept them for strangers as she says; and they say that the value of each gallon is 1½d, and so she is ordered to pay [in fines] 4s 6d.

John Redere kept the Hart, later leased to the prior of Fordham, next door to the Ram, where the Rutland Arms now stands. John Wykes, Walter Bocher and Thomas Pere all had holdings in the High Street (see plan D).

Two aletasters were appointed every year in Newmarket; they seem to have served for a couple of years at a stretch. At every court they were each fined 3d for not doing their job properly, so evidently there was either money to be made on the side or there were many more who broke the assize than are recorded on the roll. As often as not the aletasters' wives were among those fined for breaking the assize!

All in all then, providing liquid refreshment for the traveller seems to have been a flourishing Newmarket industry in the 15th century.

Travellers on this busy London to Norwich road needed not only ale but also bread, and so bakers were much in demand. At the time of the ordinance in the 13th century the price of a loaf of bread of any quality was fixed at ¼d. This meant that loaves varied in weight according to the quality of the bread. Thus a loaf of the best quality bread, known as wastel bread, weighed less than a loaf of the next quality, called cocket bread, and half the weight of a loaf of the lowest quality. A simnel loaf, perhaps the only medieval loaf still familiar to us in some form, was to weigh less than a wastel loaf because it was baked twice. The actual weight of a wastel loaf was determined by the price of wheat at the time; thus, as the ordinance states: 'when a quarter of wheat is sold for 18d, then wastel bread of a farthing, white and well baked, shall weigh £4 10s 8d' (weight was then measured in terms of coins). The ordinance goes on to list by sixpences up to £1 the cost of wheat per quarter, and the corresponding weight of a wastel loaf. The assize of bread

Illustration 9        Sixteenth century bakers at work

was meant to relate the cost of bread to the cost of wheat and to protect the consumer for whom bread was literally at this time the staff of life. Bakers were obviously tempted to charge more for a loaf and to fall short of the stipulated standards of weight and quality.

Bakers in Newmarket did not resist the temptation! Over the twelve years of our court rolls an average of twelve bakers were fined at each court, sixty different bakers in all, mostly men, for breaking the assize of bread. Although nearly all the alewives seem to have been Newmarket folk, many of the bakers seem to have come from the neighbouring villages, for example Ashley, Burwell, Bottisham, Fordham, Kentford, even Haverhill and Ely, but quite a few of those who lived in the High Street supplied bread to hungry travellers. The 15th century equivalent of our modern cafes and restaurants seems to have been supplied by communal cooks; at least ten different cooks were fined in our rolls for overcharging. All of these communal cooks seem to have lived in the High Street. Many of them were also fined for being forestallers of fish and other victuals, that is they bought before these items came into the market.

The picture of 15th century Newmarket that emerges is clearly that of a community of people largely engaged in supplying the needs of those travelling along the London-Norwich road. Probably much the same picture would emerge for the first half of the 19th century when stage coaches were a prominent feature of Newmarket life and people were coming to the town for the races.

There is little to suggest that those who lived in the High Street in the 15th century were wealthy – wealth began to flow into the town in moderate measure in the next century. Nonetheless at least one of our testators, Adam Colakyr, had an apprentice, Edmund Heyward, whom he remembered in his will; an apprentice suggests a master craftsman, with some wealth. We know further that some fifteen or more of those living in the High Street had servants, generally known simply by their Christian name, and presumably living in and doing the odd chores of house and land.

Craftsmen are occasionally mentioned. A carpenter, John Stedman, was responsible, as we have seen, for rebuilding the Tollbooth. There are many smiths, sometimes given their specific craft, for example John Balow *alias* Bladesmith. Many people's names suggest their craft, for example Gerthmaker, Souter (shoemaker), Roper, Chandler, Barker (tanner) and Saddler, but the fact that John Baker was a brasier and not a baker warns us that name and trade do not always coincide.

It is not easy to estimate what the population of Newmarket was in the 15th century. The 1472/73 account roll names fifty-five holdings; if we use a multiplier of five persons to each holding, this gives us a population of 275. Perhaps this seems rather small, but even at the end of the 17th century there were only 125 houses and a population therefore of 625, and by that time it had become 'royal' Newmarket.

## Market Means

We have already noticed that Newmarket was market based and had only one field, called sometimes the Great Common, more often Market Means; Market Means seems to be an abbreviation for the field in the (New)market (De)mesne, to distinguish it from the seven Exning fields. It seems to have covered more or less the area which we now know as Houldsworth Valley, namely the block bounded by Hamilton Road, Portland Road, Bahram Close, the line of the Upper School's playing fields below Freshfields and Rowley Drive (see plan E on page 39). It was divided into strips of varying sizes. In 1633 the parson of St Mary's had two of these strips, one of two acres and the other of half an acre, somewhere near the present Lowther Street. The other strips in this Newmarket field were cultivated by some of those who lived in the High Street.

Because Market Means was sown and harvested in common, Newmarket, like other places had strict byelaws and customs about harvesting, gleaning and the grazing of cattle. One such custom, wherever open field farming was practised, was that, while the crops were growing, cattle, sheep and pigs must be kept strictly under control and graze only the baulks that divided the separate strips. The animals were only allowed on Market

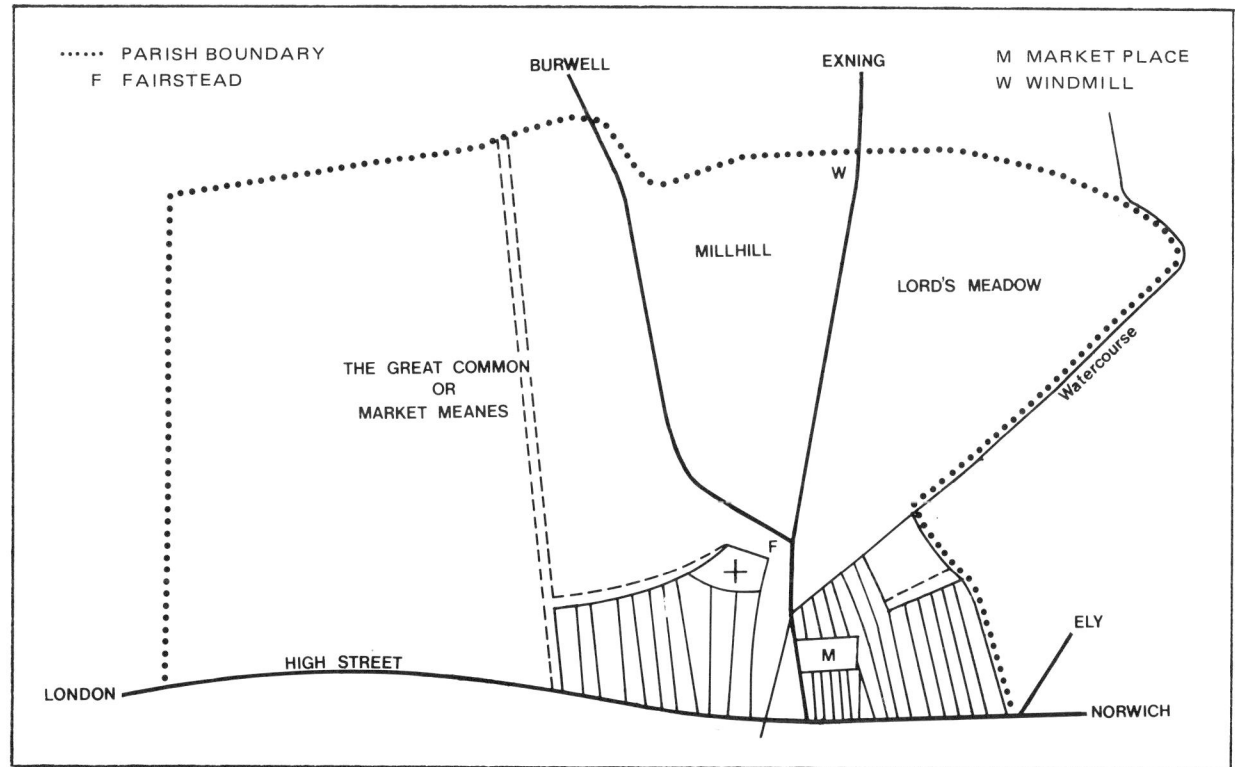

**Plan E**
**NEWMARKET (St Mary's) 1200–1500**

Means between harvesting and ploughing, and then only the animals of those who had strips in the field. The custom was of course frequently ignored, and the offenders duly fined when caught for so doing. One of the 15th century written bye-laws runs as follows:

> It is ordered by the representatives of the lords of the manor and of the tenants that all fields within the demesne of Newmarket and the Southfield of Exning up to Fabian's Head are forbidden to all sheep until St Michael's Day [29 September] and anyone who shall pasture his sheep contrary to this order shall pay to the lords 40d for each offence.

The reason for this bye-law is that sheep crop very close, and if they are allowed to graze first, there will be nothing left for the larger animals like horses and cows.

It was customary for the very young, the old and the infirm to be allowed to glean in Market Means when the harvesting had finished, but evidently able-bodied people, in Newmarket as elsewhere, habitually gate-crashed on this charitable practice. In 1403, for example, seven women were fined 3d each because they 'gleaned in the autumn and refused to work'; able-bodied people who were unwilling to work in the harvest were not expected to take advantage of the privilege of the old and infirm.

In 1407 the fine for gleaning imposed on people 'able to earn 1d a day with food' was raised to 6d. At the end of the century the practice was still going on. In 1491 gleaning was forbidden to all able-bodied people between twelve and seventy years old, the fine was increased to 2s, of which 12d went to St Mary's Church, and 12d to the lord of the manor, and informers were encouraged by an offer of 4d for each offence reported.[8]

## The Millhill

In the 15th century the Millhill covered the area bounded by St Mary's Square, Exning Road, Millbank and a now non-existent road to Burwell. John Chapman's 18th century map of Newmarket and district (now in the Jockey Club) shows a road running under what is now Freshfields to Burwell and the Swaffhams, marked possibly today by the eastern boundary of the Upper School's playing fields (see plan E on page 39). The Millhill was different from Market Means in several ways. First several of those who lived in the High Street, for example William Mey, Arthur Greysson and Katherine Poperyk (see plan E) rented land on it, over and above their strips in Market Means. Secondly the terms of their tenancies were the same as those for their holdings on fixed rents and the obligation to attend the two general courts of the manor each year. Comparison with the account roll of 1429 shows that the holdings on the High Street and land on Millhill (and elsewhere) went together. For example William Aylenoth's holding in the High Street and his rented lands correspond exactly to those held by Richard Doe in 1429. This suggests that during the 15th century there were some half a dozen of those living on the High Street who would have called themselves husbandmen, that is, smallholders, like John Grygge, mentioned earlier. In the next century they will have given themselves a rise in social status and call themselves yeomen.

Thirdly though some of the Millhill would have been arable land, the slopes of the hill had other uses. An early 17th century roll has a minute which must surely reflect a custom that goes back a century or two:

The homage [the jury of the court concerned] doe present that the herbeage of the Millhill doth belonge to the parishe of St Marye's in Newmarkett and the soyle to the lord and that the townesmen of Newmarkett weare always used to take Sand Gravell and Chalke there for their necessary uses. Butt every stranger to pay towards the church for every load 1d.[9]

When the Prior of Ely was fined 4d for digging and removing sand without the lord of the manor's permission, no doubt it was from Millhill that one of his servants took it. It may be noted that in the 19th century the eastern slopes of Millhill up to Exeter Road were called the sandpits, and Exeter Road was called Sandpit Lane.

## Lord's Meadow

The 15th century rolls of the manor all mention a ten acre field called Lord's Meadow of which the hay was sold by the lord through his bailiff to one of his tenants. This meadow seems to have been in the area between the water-course and Exning Road (see plan D). Meadow was the most valuable land of all because it provided hay as fodder for animals in winter. The hay from the ten acres of the Lord's meadow was sold for £2 a year, 4s an acre, compared with 6d an acre for rent from arable land. Nearly every year the court rolls record people trespassing in the Lord's Meadow, with their horses, cows and sheep, and twice people are fined for taking a short cut with their carts through the meadow, no doubt before the hay had been cut.

## The High Street

As we walk down the High Street today, we shall notice that, apart from two comparatively modern streets (The Avenue and Rous Road), all the roads leading off it are in effect one-way streets, too narrow for more than one car to pass at a time. On reflection we shall realise that all these lanes (for that is all they really are), Church Lane, Wellington Street, Market Street and Sun Lane, lead to centres essential to the medieval man, his church, his water supply, his mill and his market place. It may

Illustration 10
A sixteenth century scene in a High Street

Notice the piles of rubbish, the woman relieving herself, the pig browsing, the woman throwing 'water' out of the window, the inn sign and the stream running down the centre of the street.

well be then that although we have no medieval buildings (apart from St Mary's Church and that has been largely rebuilt) in Newmarket, the street pattern goes back to the middle ages.

In these days the High Street is a tidy and neat street. It is hardly likely to have been so in the 15th century. In the first place it would not have been the metalled road it is today. It would have been pitted with puddles and rutted with cart tracts and the water-course would have run across it like an open drain instead of running underground. In the second place, in the absence of council dust carts, the High Street was liable to become a dumping place for unwanted rubbish. The court rolls for 1399–1413 record many instances of this. In 1401 Roger Smith was fined 3d for blocking the High Street with a grindstone. In 1403 John Wykes, Walter Skynnere, Walter Bocher and John Manston (all but Walter Skynnere lived in the High Street) were fined for making 'goteres' in it, no doubt to draw away flood water out of their own houses. In 1400 three men were fined 1d each for putting beams of wood in the water-course in the High Street. In 1408 John Manston was ordered to remove, under threat of a fine of 3s 4d, a bank that he had constructed across the High Street, thus preventing carts from using it. Every year people were fined for throwing their refuse, night soil, dung, even butchers' entrails out into the High Street, to the nuisance of passers-by. Finally John Kyrkeby, the landlord of the Swan, was regularly fined 6d for displaying his inn sign; no doubt his inn was a single storied building and people were liable to crack their heads against it (see plan D on pages 32–33). We are reminded of the comment of a 17th century local historian, Philip Skippon:

> This Towne hath one side of the street standing in Cambridgeshire & the other side in Suffolk; when those of Suffolke goe the perambulation they passe just under the signes of Cambridgeshire side, which are all contrived so as they may with the beams the signs hang on be pulld close to the houses, else every inn forfeits a shilling to the perambulation.[10]

One holding in the High Street was the Pyndfolde or Pound, in which stray animals were impounded (see plan D). In a small area like Newmarket it cannot have often been in use. The custom seems to have been that if the animal impounded was not reclaimed by its owner within a year and a day, it became the property of the lord of the manor. At least this was what happened in the case of a stray boar in 1457.

The High Street and those who lived in it represent only half of Newmarket's story in the 15th century; the other half, the Market and those who traded in it, we must reserve for the next chapter.

## Chapter Six

## THE FIFTEENTH CENTURY:
## THE MARKET

A medieval market, in any market town, was not only a source of income to the lord of the manor, but also a centre to which people from the neighbouring villages could come to sell their produce and buy what they needed; it was also the place where craftsmen could sell their wares and merchants could obtain raw materials like timber, salt and iron. Newmarket's market seems to have fulfilled all these functions admirably. We have already seen in chapter four its contribution to the economy of the lord of the manor. We are concerned in this chapter with its role in the life of the community.

### The Market Place

It may well be that originally the market was held in the High Street — the cigar-like shape by the Post Office suggests this. But there is no doubt that by 1400 the lord of the manor had moved it off the High Street (apart from one or two stalls round the Cross) and placed it more or less where the present Rookery lies.[1] The account roll of 1472/73 calls our present Wellington Street Market Lane, implying that this lane leads off the High Street to a market place. John Chapman's 1787 *Plan of Newmarket* calls this lane Fox and Goose Lane, after an alehouse or inn whose name was changed to the Wellington after the battle of Waterloo. Our present Market Street led to a small open space, to the east of the Bushel Inn, called by him Market Place (see plan C on page 12).

What seems to have happened is that the market was moved sometime in the 14th century from the High Street to what the 25-inch O.S. Map of 1886 calls the Rookery, a clearly defined rectangle bounded by Albion Street, Market Street, Drapery Row and Wellington Street (see map F on page 44). From all accounts the old Rookery, before it was demolished some years ago, consisted of a number of narrow cobbled lanes, with numerous small dwellings, shops and public houses. It was called the Rookery not because of any connection with rooks but because its squalor suggested the mess beneath the trees of a rookery. When the market was moved there in the 14th century, it was an open rectangle on which stalls could be placed for the weekly market in the morning and removed in the evening. Little by little this area was encroached on. John Stow, in his *Survey of London* (1604) describes how this happened in London:

> These houses now possessed by Fishmongers were at the first but moveable boordes (or stalls) set out on market daies, to shew their fish there to be sold; but procuring license to set up sheds, they grew to shops, and by little and little to tall houses.[2]

We can see something of this process going on in Newmarket from the following entry in a court roll of 1409: 'John Ballowe Smyth made a window in his holding and a stall attached to the window, thus encroaching on the lord's land.'[3] He was fined the large sum of 6s 8d, but this sum may have carried with it permission to make the encroachment permanent. Thomas Pyngyll, seventy years later, had to pay 4d annually in rent for 'an empty plot lying in front of his shop, to display his merchandise on a board and not to be built on.'[4] A 15th century shop window was made of wooden boards, opening outwards to form a stall, possibly resting on trestle legs; there is an excellent example of this kind of shop front in Lavenham market place.

Eventually the open rectangle became so encroached on that by 1787 only the tiny square in John Chapman's plan was the market place, and the stalls were moved over to the High Street. There they remained until the old Rookery was demolished a few years ago, and the new Market Place was opened in the modern Rookery, more or less where it had been in the 14th century.

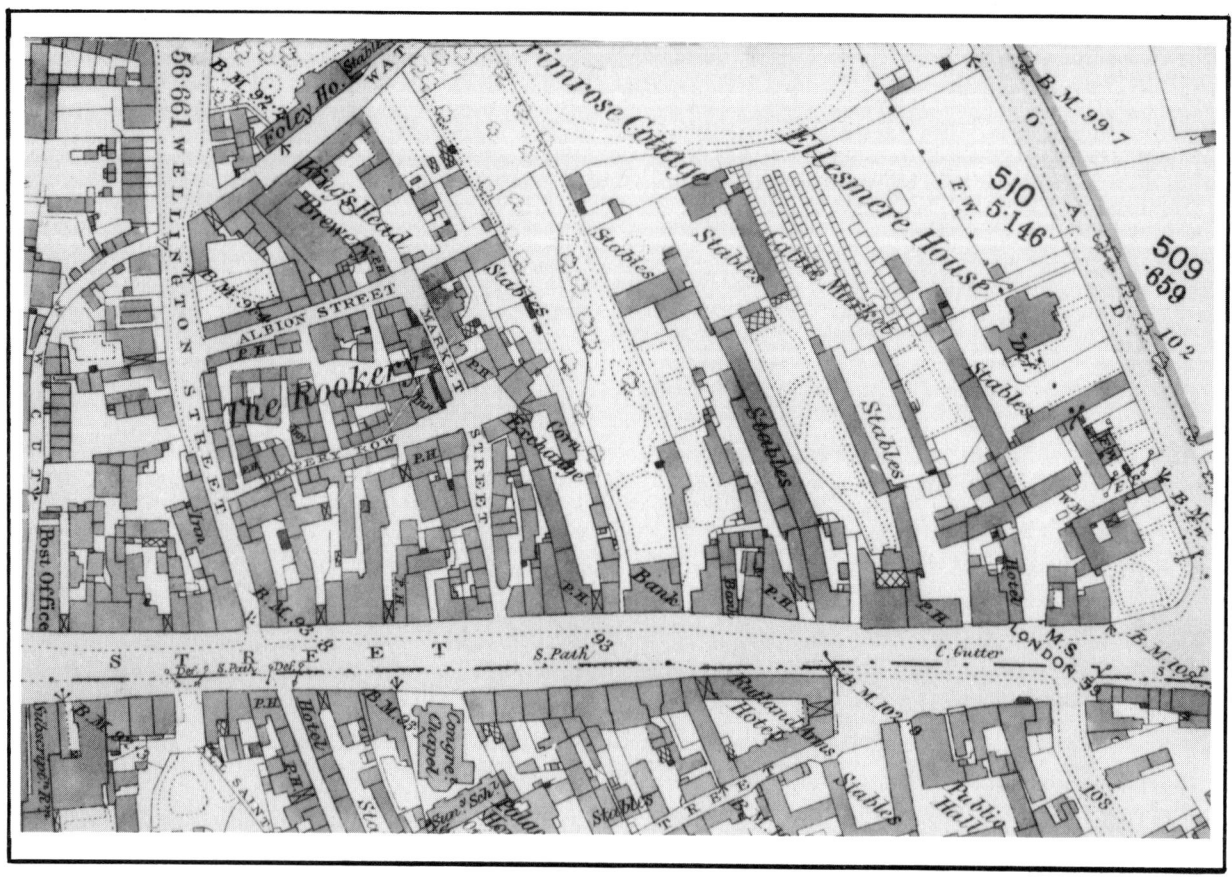

**Map F**
A section of the 25-inch O.S. Map of 1886

The 15th century market place lay in the rectangle called the Rookery enclosed by Wellington Street, Drapery Row, Market Street and Albion Street. All the poor housing shown here has been demolished and the new Rookery has taken its place.

Notice that the old county boundary ran down the south side of the High Street and not down the middle. A metal strip set in the pavement outside the present Post Office is said to mark it.

See also the note about shop signs on page 42. This suggests that Suffolk controlled the whole of the High Street except for a 'side-walk' on the south side.

In the 15th century the Icknield Way was the (Cambridgeshire) bypass running south of the High Street (see page 24 and plan D on pages 32–33).

## Shops and Stalls

The 1472/73 account roll gives a detailed list of every stall or shop held in the market, naming its then tenant (and often its previous tenant or tenants), its rent and its more or less exact location in the market place. It would be interesting to draw up a plan of the market, but the compass bearings of the scribe are somewhat confusing; we suspect that the tidy rows of our 20th century market were not for 15th century men. According to this list there were 36 stalls and 72 shops, 108 in all. The difference in theory between a stall and a shop is between a temporary and a permanent building, but in practice the roll does not observe this difference, sometimes calling the same building both stall and shop. Earlier in the 15th century the stalls and shops were arranged in rows, according to the merchandise sold in them, but by the end of the century the location of a stall in a particular row did not necessarily mean that the stallholder sold those particular goods. For example, according to the roll, John Webb *alias* Glover had to pay a pair of gloves as part of his rent, but his stall was in the Cheesemarket. The most popular row at this time was the Butchery or 'Bochery' with twenty-five shops or stalls, followed closely by the Drapery with twenty-three (the Victorian street sign 'Drapery Row' can still be seen on the wall of the Bushel Inn in the Rookery). Then come Ropers' Row, the Mercery and Barkers' (Tanners') Row with nine, Ironmongers' Row, the Cheesemarket with six and Cordwainers' Row (leatherworkers') with five shops or stalls. Several of those renting shops or stalls must have sub-let them; for example Thomas Skrevener had twenty (twelve in the Butchery) and Richard Collyng had fourteen (nine in the Drapery); earlier court rolls record cases brought by the tenant to recover rent from his sub-tenant.

The market court entries show that at the beginning of the century as later butchers played a predominant part in the market; there were Walter, Agnes, John, Richard, Nicholas, William, Thomas, Roger, Stephen, Robert and Alexander, all surnamed Bocher, as well as John Dowe, expressly described as 'bocher'. Leather workers, such as tanners and cobblers, were also prominent; there were for example Nicholas and John Sadeler, Andrew, John, Ralph, Thomas and William Barker, Thomas Souter (shoemaker) and John Gerthmaker. Perhaps it is a measure of the rise in the standard of living that retailers and middle

**Illustration 11**  **Fifteenth century butchers' shambles**

45

men such as drapers and mercers hardly appear at the beginning of the century, but by its end were playing a leading part in the market.

At the beginning of the century two other groups of traders were prominent. There appear to have been at least eight ropers trading in the market, including Thomas Roper of Fordham and William Roper of Mildenhall. One or two ropers were fined every year in the general court for selling ropes and canvas 'contrary to the statute', or, more precisely, 'by weight and not by balance'. In the early middle ages traders selling goods by weight used a type of scale called 'auncel'. According to a 1607 definition quoted in *OED*, this was a

> kind of weight with scoles [scales] hanging or hooks fastened at each end of a staffe, which a man lifted up upon his forefinger or hand and so discerneth the equalitie or difference between the weight and the thing weighed.

Since this kind of weighing depended very much on the integrity of the trader whose forefinger or hand did the balancing, 'great Damage and Deceit is done to the People'. The auncel was banned by a statute of King Edward III in 1351 which decreed that

> every Person do sell and buy by the Balance, so that the Tongue of the Balance be even, without bowing to the one side or the other, or without putting Hand or Foot or other Touch making of the same and the Wools and other Merchandises evenly weighted by the right Weight.[5]

Evidently the more unscrupulous trader in a small market like Newmarket preferred to use the banned auncel, called 'weights' in our rolls. There were also ten spicers or chandlers, including John and William Spycer of Haverhill; one or two of them were fined each year for selling their goods (oil, tar, bitumen, candles, cereals) by 'unsealed measures'.

All in all it looks as if our traders served the local community with goods essential for daily living and did not deal very much in luxury goods, on sale perhaps in the fairs rather than markets. The Cornhill, somewhere near the Bushel Inn, is mentioned frequently in the rolls, so presumably people came to the market to sell and buy cereals. There is no indication that it was at any time in this century a cattle or sheep market.

A trader had to pay an entry fee on taking over the tenancy of a stall or shop in the market, as the following entry in a court roll for 1409 shows:

> To this court came Richard Farewel [a butcher from Ashley] and remitted and released to Robert Gateward [a tanner] all rights and claims that he has or in any way could have in 2 shops, namely 1 shop in the 'lyndraperye' next to the said Robert Gateward's shop, and the other shop lies next to the lord's land. To be held to him [Robert Gateward] and his heirs by the rod at the will of the lord according to the custom of the manor. And he paid the entry fee of 2s.[6]

The phrase 'by the rod' refers apparently to the fact that a white rod was held out to a new tenant as a sign that he could now take possession of the property concerned. The lease for such shops was for a period of years, perhaps twenty, not for the life of the tenant, and the rent could be raised and indeed was raised when the lord so wished, although the custom of the manor may well by this time have curtailed his powers in this direction.

A trader had also of course to pay his annual rent, ranging in 1472/73 from 4d to 3s. If we disregard the fifteen shops and stalls which carried an annual rent of 2s or more, the average rent for the remaining ninety-three stalls and shops was just over 5d a year, of which the greater number were at 4d, apparently the standard rate. Of the fifteen rated at 2s or over, three were beside the Tollbooth, clearly a coveted and valuable site; John Pyrton had to pay 6s 8d for the shop on its eastern side and John Whityng 5s 6d for that on the western.

The trader in the market had also to pay a toll to the lord of the manor on all food (and perhaps other items) sold. An entry in a court roll for 1403 records how John Fabyan (surely from Exning) was fined 6d because 'on the Tuesday next before the feast of St Peter ad Vincula [1 August] he struck the lord's bailiff and refused to pay the tax of a farthing on four bushels of barley.'[7] Evasion of this tax by what was called 'forestalling' was common; traders sold their wares *before* actually coming into the market place and setting up their stalls. Fines for such evasions were frequently imposed in the general court, particularly for the sale of meat and fish (including on occasion oysters). Many of these forestallers were not strictly traders in the market but were residents in the High Street, using their own houses to sell what they had bought. Some of those who had holdings in the High Street backing on the market place had a permit or licence from the lord of the manor to have their doors open on to the market. This privilege was abused by others; for example John Higham who had two holdings backing on to the market place, the Sword and the Pyndfolde (see plan D on pages 32–33) was fined 2s in 1411 because he had no such permit, and was ordered to close his door in future.[8]

In all that we have said so far, Newmarket differed very little from other 15th century market towns. In one respect it was however unusual, almost unique; it had a market court.

## The Market Court

In all the thousands of pre-16th century court rolls listed in the *Index of Court Rolls* in the Public Record Office in Chancery Lane, there are only thirteen places whose market court rolls are alleged to have survived. On examination almost all of these are in fact concerned not with markets but with fairs.[9] The legislative problems connected with fairs, held once or twice a year, are clearly quite different in many respects from those connected with markets, held at least once a week. We are fortunate in having preserved for us the market court rolls for the manor of Newmarket from 1399 till 1413.[10]

The market court at Newmarket was in theory a court to which traders in the market could bring suits for debt, trespass, detention of goods etc against fellow traders in the market. It was always held therefore on market day, then as now Tuesday, generally every second or third Tuesday, since there was normally not sufficient business for a weekly meeting. In effect however it was a debtors' court; out of the 338 cases recorded in the rolls 286 or

84.6 per cent were concerned with debt. Once we have realised this, we can observe that its main concern, the collection of debts, was dealt with in other manors at other courts among other business, usually the general court or as it is sometimes called the court baron. In these courts however a creditor was only able normally to recover what was due to him if he and his debtor belonged to the same manor.

What was unusual about Newmarket's market court was that it provided a service which cut across manorial boundaries, and in effect became a court in which anyone, trader or not, could bring a suit against anyone else, trader or not, wherever either of them belonged. A good example of this is the case of Maliard *versus* Wynde in 1405. John Maliard was evidently the lord of a manor at East Dereham in Norfolk. He sued John Wynde of Bury St Edmunds, his estate agent, in the Newmarket market court, for 10 marks (about £7) due to him (John Maliard) when John Wynde's accounts were audited. Neither of them could be described as traders in the market at Newmarket, nor were they tenants under the jurisdiction of its manor. Presumably the market court at Newmarket was chosen by John Maliard for his suit because it provided an extra-manorial service, and was a convenient distance from both Bury St Edmunds and East Dereham. There appear to have been places, strategically placed, at least in East Anglia, for example the Barton Gate at Ely and Sudbury, where such cases, not necessarily concerned with markets but butting across manorial boundaries and available for anyone, could be heard.[11]

Of course the majority of cases heard in the market court at Newmarket are between people living in its vicinity, but it is surprising how many and from how far people came to the market court to settle their differences. Plan G on page 49 shows how far afield they came. Beyond its range were William of Banbury, Thomas Fyschere of Bedford, John Bocher and John Coteler of Thaxted, Walter Tennison of Newport Pagnell and Thomas Clyff of King's Lynn (then known as Lynn Episcopi or Bishop's Lynn). If we add to this list surnames which *may* indicate a place of origin, such as Robert

Peterborough, Robert Grantham, Richard Dunmow and Thomas Harlow, the scope and importance of the market and its court at Newmarket appears remarkable.

As we have seen, nearly 85 per cent of the cases heard in the court were concerned with debt, occasionally large but for the most part small. One of the larger cases was that brought by William Chevele, the steward of the manor, against William Ray. He sued William in August 1412 for £6 2s 6d due to him for wool sold by him on 24 June 1411; as that day was a Wednesday and not therefore market day, evidently the sale did not take place at the market, but William Chevele could nonetheless bring his suit to the market court. William Ray had to pledge his three shops in the market as pledge that he would pay the debt and the court fee if he lost the case.

The items pledged by defendants and valued by fellow stallholders in the market give some indication of their social status and wealth. By far the most frequently pledged item (39 per cent) was a horse, presumably offered or demanded as the trader's means of transport from market to market. After trading in Newmarket on Tuesday, he could move to Bury St Edmunds on Wednesday, to Ely on Thursday and to Soham or Mildenhall on Friday. 10.4 per cent of pledges were in the form of meat and 7.5 per cent in that of leather goods, reflecting, what we have already noticed, the prominent part taken in the market by butchers and leather workers.

Other pledged items such as a tunic, tubs, andirons, a griddle, a sickle, 'pakkes' and articles essential for an inn show that others besides traders used the market court to recover debts from ordinary citizens, some of them by no means well-to-do.

The suits for the recovery of debts make rather monotonous reading. Occasionally we come across cases of interest. For instance in 1407 Richard Derlyng sued Thomas atte Hel for selling him a horse guaranteed to be sound in wind and limb, but which, Richard claimed, did not merit this description. The court ordered Thomas to come to the next court with five others who would vouch for his integrity; he was not able to do so and lost the case. In 1408 Laurence Horn sued John Baxtere for damages of 3s 4d for selling him a brass pot which Laurence claimed to be made of lead. The jury awarded him damages of 4d only, judging that the pot concerned was indeed of brass but had been badly cast.

Human nature has not changed all that in nearly 600 years.

---

Plan G — Key

| 1 | Moulton | 21 | Teversham |
|---|---|---|---|
| 2 | Gazeley | 22 | Quy |
| 3 | Higham | 23 | Bottisham |
| 4 | Barrow | 24 | Willingham |
| 5 | Stetchworth | 25 | Swaffham |
| 6 | Cheveley | 26 | Reach |
| 7 | Ashley | 27 | Burwell |
| 8 | Dalham | 28 | Exning |
| 9 | Ousden | 29 | Snailwell |
| 10 | Lidgate | 30 | Chippenham |
| 11 | Kirtling | 31 | Fordham |
| 12 | Cowlinge | 32 | Freckenham |
| 13 | Barnardiston | 33 | Soham |
| 14 | Hundon | 34 | Mildenhall |
| 15 | Kedington | 35 | Eriswell |
| 16 | Great Wratting | 36 | Cavenham |
| 17 | Balsham | 37 | Thurlow |
| 18 | Carlton | 38 | Withersfield |
| 19 | Brinkley | 39 | Kennett |
| 20 | Wilbraham | | |

*From outside the 16-mile radius:*

| | |
|---|---|
| Banbury | Mendlesham |
| Bedford | Feltwell |
| Hoxne | Grantham |
| Thaxted | Peterborough |
| Botesdale | Halesworth |
| Oxeforth (Oxford?) | Diss |
| St Neot's | Dunmow |
| South Elmham | Bumstead |
| King's Lynn (Lynn Episcopi) | Newport Pagnell |
| East Dereham | Sutton |

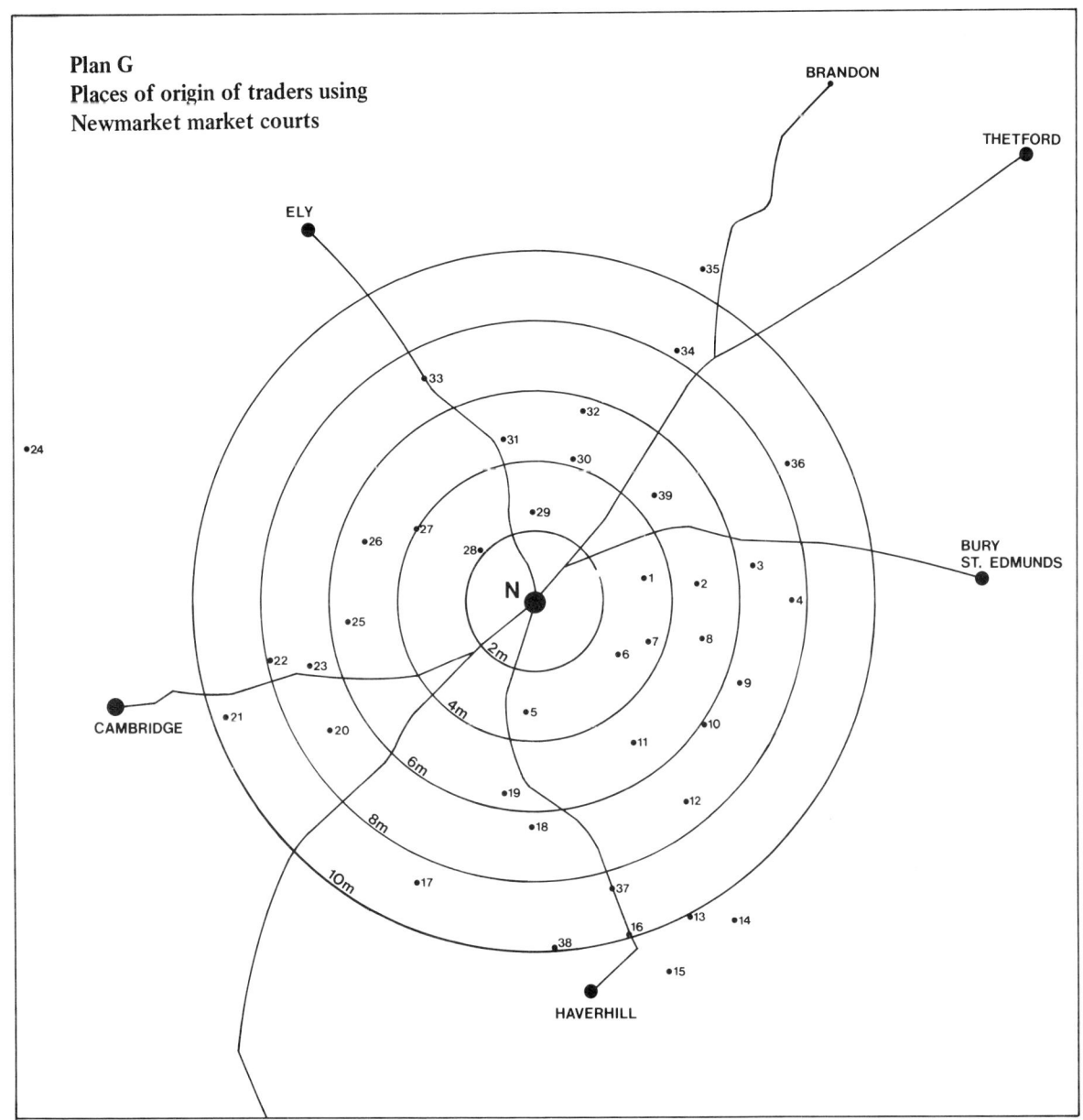

**Plan G**
**Places of origin of traders using**
**Newmarket market courts**

BRANDON

THETFORD

ELY

BURY
ST. EDMUNDS

CAMBRIDGE

HAVERHILL

N

2m
4m
6m
8m
10m

## The Pie-powder Court

Most of the cases heard in the market court were initiated at one meeting of the court and heard at a meeting a fortnight or so later. But Newmarket, like other places, had what was called a 'pie-powder' court (so called from the French *pieds poudrés* meaning dusty feet). A plaintiff could ask for his case to be heard there and then, not only because he might need his money immediately but also because the defendant might be an itinerant peddler who might not appear again for some months. An excellent example of our Newmarket pie-powder court was the suit brought by John Magote in 1399. He sued Richard Drover for 7s 4d; if Richard was what his name implies, then he was probably passing through Newmarket with his cattle. The court seized as pledge what appear to be all Richard's possessions, namely a coverlet (valued at 2s), a blanket (12d), a white jacket (4d), a cradle cloth (nil), six white skins (6d), a chest or coffer (12d), two small plates (10d), a cushion (1d), three purses (1d), three razors (2d), a sack with a wallet (4d) and a horse with saddle (12d). Although he was 'cried' (presumably by Newmarket's equivalent of a town crier) five times during the all-day sitting of the court, he did not appear and John Magote was awarded all his bits and pieces, out of which he had to realise 12d to pay to the court for bringing the case.

## High Street and Market

We may perhaps have given the impression that High Street and Market did not often mix; there were of course some who had their feet in both camps. One of them was Simon Funston who died in 1497. He had three shops in the market place and three houses situated somewhere between the market place and the watercourse, perhaps where the Astley Institute now is. One of these houses was called 'the old Bakehouse' and had a barn and stable. Another was called 'Fannefeyre'; perhaps this was an inn. (For the location of these houses see plan D on pages 32–33). He also leased from the lord of the manor seven acres of demesne land, lying to the west of the Exning road. In his will he left to 'Margarett my wyff al my londes houses croftes & medowes in whatt town or felde thatt they hap at be in the terme of her lyff'. If we may judge from his bequests to the 'chyrche werkes' of Cheveley, Woodditton and All Saints', Newmarket, it was probably in the fields of these 'towns' that he had his lands. His son Henry, to whom he left a horse, is described in a lease of 1533 as a yeoman of Woodditton.[12]

Perhaps Simon's chief claim to fame in Newmarket is that he was the founder of a family which was to play a prominent part in the life of the town for the next 200 years.

Another who had interests in both High Street and Market was Ralph Lote *alias* Taylor. As plan D shows, he had *previously* been tenant of holdings occupied in 1472/73 by John Grygge (49 and 53), Roger Holyngworth (50), Henry Dale (54) and John Glover (55), and was still renting two holdings on either side of Market Lane (12 and 13) and a holding between the Bull and the Saracen's Head on the other side of the High Street, then in Cambridgeshire (41). What is perhaps even more significant is that he had previously rented (but no longer did so) a stall in the Butchery, a shop in the Drapery, a stall in front of the Cross in the High Street and five out of the nine stalls in Barkers' Row. So perhaps he had made his money in the tanning business, in spite of his *alias* Taylor and then gone into property which presumably he sub-let.[13]

In conclusion our brief survey of Newmarket's market and its market court during the 15th century has shown us that it had an important role to play in providing essential goods and a measure of justice to the surrounding villages and even towns.

## Chapter Seven

# THE SIXTEENTH CENTURY

Probably the 16th century is the period of our history most familiar and also most attractive to the majority of English people, familiar because of King Henry VIII and his wives, Mary Queen of Scots, good Queen Bess and the Spanish Armada, attractive because of robust characters like Sir Walter Raleigh, Sir Francis Drake and Sir Thomas More. These are unlikely to have had much impact except incidentally on the 250—300 inhabitants of a small market town like Newmarket. Statutes passed at Westminster which had to be implemented locally, the continual demand for financial subsidies from the nation, and the rise in the cost of living (apparently trebling between 1500 and 1600) are reflected much more in local documents.[1] And we must add of course the traumatic experience of the Reformation. We shall look at the effect of these on Newmarket later in the chapter.

## A Case of Defamation

The century opens however with two incidents which must have caused excitement and alarm in our town. First in 1502 Thomas Depden took John Withall to the Norwich Diocesan Consistory Court for defamation of character. A glance at the plan of Newmarket in 1472 (see pages 32—33) will show that Thomas Depden had three holdings in Newmarket. Two of these were on the north side of the town, including the Bear, for which he had to pay the large sum of 9s 5d annually to the lord of the manor. The other was on the south side of the High Street and was on the rent roll of the manor of Woodditton. It was in the courtyard of this house at about 3 o'clock in the afternoon of 10 December 1501

that John Withall burst out in anger: 'Thomas Depden was a False man and made a false Writyng', apparently about the transfer of property. John Withall was a comparative newcomer to Newmarket, but he was a well-to-do man, landlord of the Ram (the modern Rutland Arms), with another house called 'the Shoppes' as well as land in Cambridgeshire and Suffolk. So on 4 June 1502 Thomas Depden went to the Diocesan Consistory Court at Norwich to clear his name. He produced three witnesses alleged to have been present when John Withall uttered the offensive words. Although all three were illiterate, they were free men and so their evidence was admissable in court. They all claimed to have known Thomas Depden and John Withall well for many years and swore on oath that they had heard John utter the defamatory words or similar.[2] Unfortunately the findings of the court have not been preserved, so we do not know its decision.

Thomas Depden died in 1517 at Sudbury, and in his will asked to be buried before the statue of St Peter in St Gregory's church. He appears to have been a somewhat solitary man, for he had no wife or children to whom to leave his property, and his only personal bequest was to his servant, Margaret Mylner. Although he recognised his obligations to the two churches in Newmarket, there is no mention in his will of his property there, so it may well be that he lost his case against John Withall, sold up and went off to end his days in Sudbury.

John Withall died in 1524, giving generously in his will to All Saints' Church, to the four orders of friars at Cambridge and to the prior and convent at Fordham (the prior of Fordham was landlord of the Hart next door to the Ram). He left 20s to be spent in the 'reparation of the way called Hiklingswey leading from the tenement called the Rame in Newmarket towards the Church of All Saints', what we call today Palace Street. He also gave, rather unusually, 20s for a gravestone to be placed over his grave in All Saints' churchyard with the words engraven (in Latin): 'Pray for the souls of John Withall and his wives Margaret and Joan'; Joan was his second wife and was still alive.[3] His bequests in general suggest a more outgoing and happier man than Thomas Depden.

## A Take-over Bid?

The other incident which must have alarmed the people of Newmarket at the beginning of the 16th century was what appears to have been a take-over bid from one of the manors of Exning, probably Cotton Manor. It was claimed that the one Newmarket field, Market Means, which we have mentioned earlier (see plan D on pages 32–33), did not belong to the manor of Newmarket at all, but was really part of Exning. Concerned and threatened Newmarket folk were able to produce three pieces of evidence to refute the Exning claim. First Market Means was operated on quite different lines from the seven fields of Exning in that, unlike them, it never lay fallow and that those who had strips in it worked on saints' days and Exning folk took the day off. Secondly the 'Townschipe' of Exning had to pay £5 a year to the sheriff of Suffolk for its fields while Newmarket had to pay nothing, a payment that may date back to the 12th century when Exning was transferred from Cambridgeshire to Suffolk. Thirdly entries were produced from the court rolls of the manor of Newmarket to show that for at least 100 years the lords of the manor of Newmarket had had jurisdiction over Market Means. The field remained Newmarket's.[4]

It is interesting to speculate why Exning should have made a claim like this; was it because Newmarket had originally been carved out of Exning? Or was it because manorial jurisdiction in Newmarket had grown slack over the years? Or was it because the whole pattern of Newmarket life had become so urban that its residents were no longer particularly interested in their strips in Market Means? It may well have been the latter because, as we shall see, there is a certain amount of evidence that retailers and innholders rather than yeomen were now taking the lead in Newmarket.

## The Gentry

Television programmes have made us familiar with the elegant manners and clothes of the courtiers and gentry associated with King Henry VII and Queen Elizabeth. Courtiers had of course passed through Newmarket for centuries, but they only came to stay after King James I had discovered it. The Alingtons as lords of the manor were the gentry most likely to be associated with Newmarket but they lived at Horseheath. I can find only two gentry mentioned in this century at Newmarket, neither of whom seems to have played any part in its life. John Crickmer's daughter, Frances, married Richard Hamerton who at the end of the century had the lease of the Griffin, later to become the site of the King's Palace; Richard himself, in 1608, became the first 'keeper of the king's house' at Newmarket. Thomas Stooks is the only other person described as a gentleman in Newmarket in the 16th century. He was from Norwich and owned in Newmarket the Stonehouse, so called because houses made of stone were rare outside of the larger towns. It was on the Heath at the western end of the town, and must have been somewhere near the White Lion, opposite the Dullingham Road. Thomas Stooks appears neither to have lived in it nor kept it in good repair. It was however one of the prestigious houses in Newmarket — we can trace its owners from Thomas Stooks' time to the 1830s when it was occupied by Stephen Piper, the leading brewer of the time.

The only suggestion of the country pursuits in which 16th century gentry delighted is John Ayers' bequest in 1558 of 'one couple of my best hounds to John Alington' and three best 'dogges' to Sir Giles Alington.[5] But as he himself lived in the Sword and his brother David described himself as a yeoman, he was probably enjoying the pursuits of the gentry without himself being one.

The situation was quite different in the next century when James I and Charles II brought their courts to Newmarket for their social activities. Accommodation in the palace buildings was limited, and a living-out allowance was paid to those gentlemen of the court for whom there was no room. The frequent mention of gentlemen in the court rolls suggests that some of them, like their Edwardian successors, bought, perhaps built, second homes in which they could stay when in Newmarket. Such arrangements were unthinkable in the 16th century.

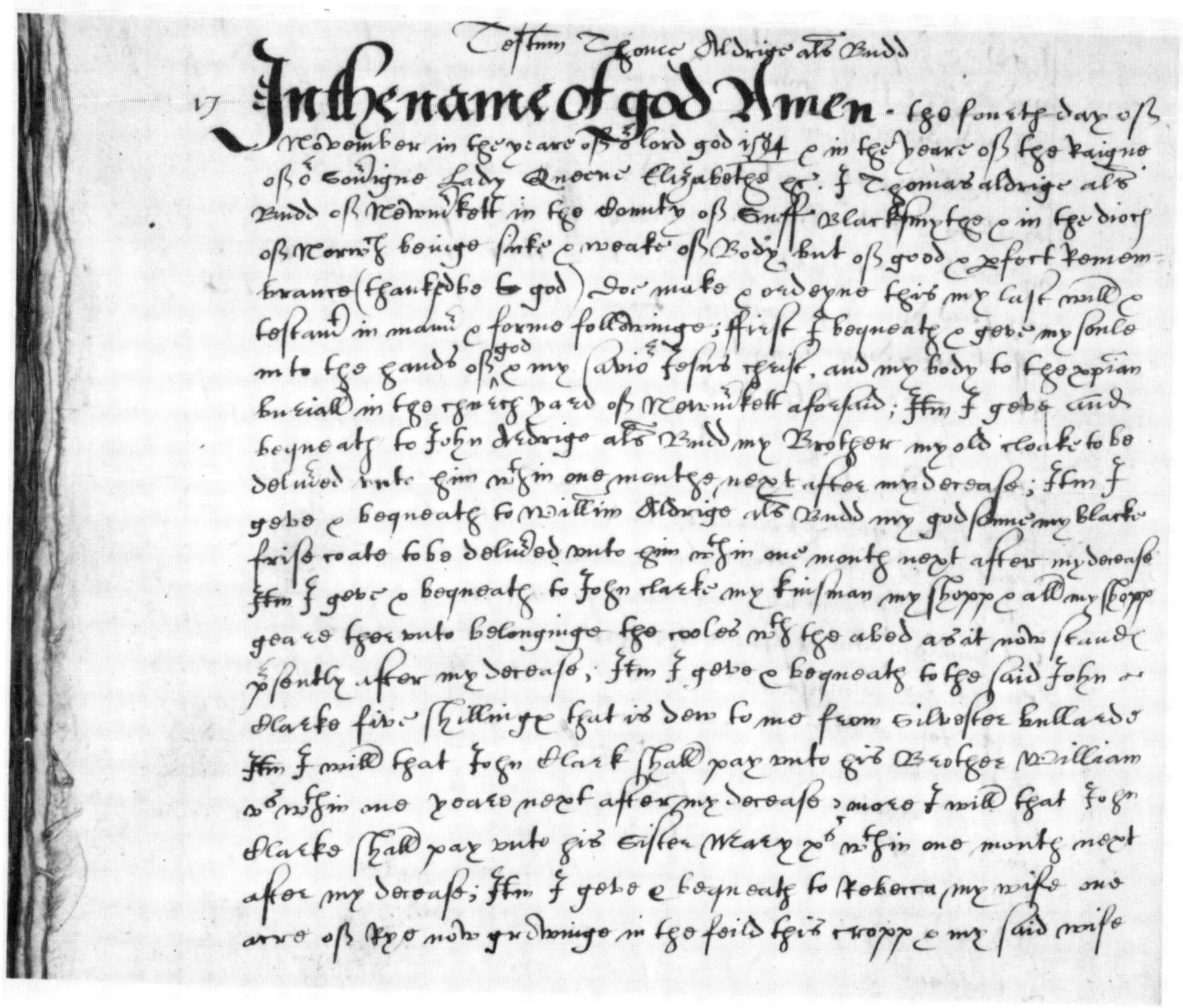
Testm Thome Aldrige als Budd
17 In the name of god Amen - the fourth day of Novembre in the yeare of our lord god 1594 & in the yeare of the raigne of our soveraigne Lady Queene Elizabethe &c. I Thomas aldrige als Budd of Newmarkett in the County of Suff Blacksmythe & in the dioc of Norwich beinge sicke & weake of Body but of good & perfect remembrance (thankes be to god) doe make & ordeyne this my last will & testament in manner & forme followinge; ffirst I bequeathe & geve my soule unto the handes of god & my savior Jesus Christ, and my body to christian buriall in the church yard of Newmarkett aforesaid; Item I geve and bequeath to John Aldrige als Budd my Brother my old cloake to be delivered unto him wthin one monthe next after my decease; Item I geve & bequeath to William Aldrige als Budd my godsonne my blacke frise coate to be delivered unto him wthin one month next after my decease Item I geve & bequeath to John Clarke my kinsman my shopp & all my shopp geare therunto belonginge the cooles wth the abed as it now standes presently after my decease, Item I geve & bequeath to the said John Clarke five shillinges that is dew to me from Silvester Bullarde Item I will that John Clark shall pay unto his Brother William xs within one yeare next after my decease; more I will that John Clarke shall pay unto his Sister Mary xs wthin one month next after my decease; Item I geve & bequeath to Rebecca my wife one acre of Rye now growinge in the feild this cropp & my said wife

**Illustration 12**
**An extract from the will of Thomas Aldrige *alias* Budd, 1594**

**Thomas Aldrige was a blacksmith. In his will he bequeaths to his kinsman, John Clarke (see lines 14ff), his 'shopp' (i.e. his forge), all his 'shopp geare therunto belonginge', the 'cooles' (coals) and the 'abed' (anvil?). Notice also that he leaves to his wife Rebecca an acre of rye 'now growinge in the feild [i.e. Market Means] this cropp'.**

## Yeomen

The next rung down the social ladder was that of yeoman. Yeomen have been described as a rural middle class, making their way by diligent application to their holdings in land. Some twenty people in 16th century Newmarket so call themselves, and some of them certainly merit the description; for others it seems to have been a mark of social status rather than of function.

According to the assessments for lay subsidies to the Crown made between 1545 and 1600, only one person in Newmarket could be described in this period as wealthy. Thomas Dove, a yeoman, alone had his goods and land assessed at more than £40. When he died in 1548 he left all his lands in the (Cambridgeshire) fields of Newmarket, Woodditton, Saxton and Cheveley and five acres of land in the fields of Exning to his son Thomas, all his houses and land in Wratting to his son John, and 'my house in Newmarket lying next the church lane with 2 single half acres of land lying in the [market] meanes in the county of Suffolk' to his son William. Besides this he was able to bequeath £20 to each of his three sons and two daughters when they reached the age of twenty, as well as half a dozen silver spoons to each of his daughters.[6] Clearly his main interest in life had been in farming his land and he had used the profits from them not in extravagant spending but in providing for his family.

Nearly 75 per cent of those assessed in Newmarket for lay subsidies in the 16th century were in the wealth bracket £2—£10, what may be described as lower middle class. It was this class which dominated 16th century Newmarket. Walter Button, assessed at £4, was probably a typical member of it. In his will he describes himself as yeoman, but this was probably his own claim to status. When he died in 1594 he left to his wife Agnes his house called the Chequer (evidently on the Suffolk side of the High Street), fourteen acres of land in the fields of Exning and his copyhold shops in Newmarket. He also left a coomb of malt or rye to at least twenty other people including two coombs of wheat and two coombs of rye to the poor of Newmarket 'to be baked and given

at my charge'. His four daughters each were to receive £20 when they reached the age of twenty-one.[7] But in the court rolls for 1577—1583 he was fined on three counts: as a baker because he broke the assize of bread, as an alehouse keeper (no doubt at the Chequer), and as a retailer whose charges were excessive. He was clearly using his fourteen acres to develop other lines of business, and can hardly be described as a typical yeoman. His son, another Walter, continued in his father's tradition. To what he had inherited from his father through his mother when she died, he added three shops in the market place and another alehouse, the Half Moon (in the 19th century this was where Jackson-Stops and Staff have their business at 168 High Street).[8]

An example of the diversification of a yeoman's interests may be seen in the mention of saffron grounds or 'pans' in four of the wills made in the 16th century. For instance in the will of Joan Best, widow of John Best, yeoman, in 1541, we find the following: 'as touching my saffron grounds John Chaundelour my brother to have one pan and Thomas Regewell another pan and Thomas Turner that shall next be raised.'[9] For what was the saffron *(crocus sativus)* being grown? For cooking, for example for cakes at bride-ales and thanksgivings for women, and also for the value it was thought to have for medicinal purposes. William Bullein in his *Booke of Simples*, published in 1562, declares the virtues of saffron thus:

This Safron is commonly knowen here in Englande, bothe in Norfolke, Cambridgeshire, and Essex etc., [a chalky subsoil being particularly suited for its growth] with purple flowers, with yellowe small Chives: and heddes growyng in the grounde, wherein be cloves of yerely increase. . . . Assuredly, there is no better safron in Europe. . . . It doe warme, make soft, digeste, provoke urin, make good colour in the face. It comforteth the hart, and defendeth dronkenes: moveth Venus. . . . Safron is good against al maner of swellyng in the breaste, winde in the bellie and guttes: and stoppyng of the moth of the matrix, either in ointment, or drinke. It is a good cordiall, to be used in meates, of melancholie persons: to rejoice thee, and make glad a weake harte.[10]

Saffron fetched a good price in the market, 12s being paid for a pound in 1545 and 30s in 1588. Farming of it ceased round about 1790 when it was realised that its medicinal properties were greatly exaggerated.[11]

A house typical of a small yeoman living in Newmarket during the 16th century might well be that of John Thomson. When he died in 1576 his goods and chattels were valued for probate by five of his neighbours who went from room to room, listing what he had in each of them. It seems clear that he was a yeoman, or at least a husbandman, for he had four horses and a cart and gear in his stables, five 'hogges', six 'pigges' and eleven 'fowles' in his yards, £10 worth of hay in his 'oslry', and nine acres of corn growing in the fields as well as three and a half acres lying fallow. His house was three storied. On the ground floor was his hall or living room and his kitchen, full of the usual cooking vessels. On the first floor were two chambers or bedrooms over the hall and the kitchen, and on the second floor another bedroom called the upper chamber. To judge from the amount of furniture in all five rooms, there cannot have been much room to move about in. He seems to have had a large family, for in his three bedrooms were three posted beds (that is 'four posters'), three truckle beds that could be rolled under the posters and four boarded beds (that is with solid panels at the head or at both ends), with twenty-two pairs of sheets for them; no question of single bedrooms in his house! All his goods and chattels were valued at £43 16s 4d, worth of course many times as much today. Half of this wealth lay in his horses, his hay and the products of his twelve and a half acres, as one might expect of a small yeoman.[12]

The lists of those Newmarket people assessed to contribute to lay subsidies for Queen Elizabeth give us some indication of their occupations. The list for the Cambridgeshire side of Newmarket for 1562/63 has fifteen names, consisting of three yeomen, two fishmongers, two (ale?)house holders, a mercer, a grocer, a wheelwright, a baker, a draper, a peddler, an innkeeper and an 'alien' (elsewhere described as an alehouse keeper).[13] The list for the Suffolk side for 1581/82 has eighteen names, including nine alehouse keepers or innkeepers, of whom some were also bakers or brewers or retailers.[14] One was a shoemaker. All but one of the rest are described elsewhere as retailers. The only one whose occupation we do not know is Jeremy Halfhead. He however lived in Saffron Walden and had inherited shops and land in Newmarket from his mother-in-law — he had married the daughter of John Kyrbie, a tanner sufficiently wealthy to be able to employ two apprentices.[15]

**Illustration 13**                    **Sixteenth century shoemakers at work**

Illustration 14
A fourteenth century tavern scene
(Italian)

## Inns and Alehouses

The frequent mention of inns and alehouses suggests that 16th century Newmarket people were continuing the role of their 15th century forefathers in supplying the needs of travellers on the London to Norwich road. There were differences however. We saw in Chapter Five what a large part alewives played in the supply of liquid refreshment in the 15th century and how many were regularly fined for breaking the assize of ale. By the middle of the 16th century they have completely disappeared. In the courts of 1577–1583 only nine different people were fined for breaking the assize, all of them men and six of them alehouse keepers or innholders. All told in these years there were at least thirteen alehouses or inns. It is not always easy to determine whether the house mentioned is an inn or merely a drinking house. Certainly the Ram (now the Rutland Arms) and the Saracen's Head were inns and probably the Griffin (of which more later). The Star (on the corner of Sun Lane where today Peatling and Cawdron have their business) sounds more like a doss-house than an inn: in 1595 John Hudson the landlord was fined 40s for harbouring paupers there contrary to a Newmarket bye-law. Others known to us by name in the 16th century are the Sword, the Half Moon, the Greyhound (on the south side of the High Street, somewhere between Sun Lane and the Jockey Club), the Crown (on the site of the present Crown at 28 High Street?), the Angel, the Chequer, the George, the Two Lyames (Limes?) and the Maidenhead (see plan D on pages 32–33).

The selling of wine was different from that of ale. In 1552/53 a statute of King Edward VI prohibited the licensing of more than two taverns in any town for the sale of wine retail or wholesale. Larger towns were excepted; for example London was allowed forty, York eight, Cambridge and Norwich four and Ipswich three.[16] Only one licence was granted to Newmarket, to Leonard and Margaret Beale.[17] The tavern where they sold their wines was the Griffin. There they remained, leasing it to Richard Hamerton, until 1608, when King James I chose it and the houses around it for the palace complex. Leonard Beale was paid £10 a year as reserved rent and up to £400 for its purchase.[18] The Griffin had been one of Newmarket's major inns for nearly 200 years — it is mentioned in Edward Baron's will of 1439. With the building of the Palace at the beginning of the 17th century it disappears from the scene.

In Chapter Five we saw what a large part bakers played in supplying the needs of travellers and how many of them were fined for breaking the assize of bread. Like the alewives they have virtually disappeared by the end of the 16th century. Over the years 1577–1583 only eight different men were fined for breaking it. The major offence during these years was that of excessive profiteering by retailers, especially perhaps victuallers. Over thirty people a year were fined for this offence. It goes back to a statute of King Edward III in 1349 by which

> Butchers, Fishmongers, Hostelers, Brewers, Bakers, Pulters and other sellers of all manner of Victuals shall be bound to sell the same Victual for a reasonable Price, having respect to the Price that such Victual be sold at the Places adjoining, so that the same Sellers have moderate Gains and not excessive, reasonably to be required according to the distance of the Place from whence the said Victuals be carried.[19]

## Retailers and Craftsmen

What of the market? The court rolls of the latter half of the century record the transfer of shops from one tenant to another. It is significant that the word 'stall' (a temporary erection) is never used; the transfer is always of shops (a more permanent building). It seems clear that the encroachment to which we referred in Chapter Six had been going on apace, apparently encouraged by the lord of the manor, who on one occasion leased a piece of waste lane in the market place on condition that the tenant built a shop on it within two years. Another indication of encroachment is the reference on several occasions to workshops, that is shops in which work and retailing were combined. These would seem to be more permanent buildings in which craftsmen could store their tools, work at their craft and sell their goods.

Christopher Roughe, for example, a cobbler, had a holding next to the Sword in the High Street (see plan D on pages 32–33). His workshop was behind his holding on Market Hill (hill here indicating the place where the market was held, as in Cornhill); there he kept his shop gear, leather lasts, shoes etc, which he instructed his executor in his will to sell for, among other things, the education of his children.[20] There was also a workshop on the west side of the Tollbooth. Some of those who had shops in the town were undoubtedly retailers. John Murdun, a draper, whose inventory we have produced on page 60, may well be typical of his class.[21] When

**Illustration 15**      **Sixteenth century blacksmiths at work**

he died in 1576 his goods and chattels were valued at £40 6s 3d, much the same as John Thomson's, at whose inventory we looked earlier in this chapter. Half John Murdun's wealth lay in his shop, in which he had shelves, chests and cloth valued at £20, with £5 due to him in debts. If his house conformed to a standard pattern observed elsewhere in towns, it was three storied. On the ground floor were his shop (with its front on the High Street) and the 'backhouse', a backroom opening on to his yard where he kept his 'hoges' and 'poltre'. On the first floor were his hall or living room, his kitchen and his 'butre' (really only a store cupboard), and on the second floor was the (bed)chamber, probably under the eaves and extending over the hall and the kitchen below. We have to remember that frontage on a town high street was valuable, and houses there tended to extend backwards rather than sideways. John Murdun's house may have been as typical of Newmarket's retailers as John Thomson's of its small yeomen.

Retailers such as drapers, chandlers, grocers and mercers, and craftsmen such as blacksmiths (see John Aldrige's will on page 53), coopers, glovers, leather workers, cobblers and wheelwrights, all played their part in the life of Newmarket in the 16th century, contributing by their skills to the needs of the town, the neighbouring villages and travellers.

We must not forget those who had always played a dominant part in the market, namely the butchers, or 'fleshers' as they were sometimes called. Twenty-seven of them were fined in the court of 1580 for making excessive profits. References to shops in the butchery and to the butchers' shambles (slaughterhouse) are often found in 16th century wills and court rolls. Surprisingly again fishmongers are mentioned, John Bullard and John King being wealthy enough to have to pay subsidies to Queen Elizabeth in 1562/63.

The court appointed every year constables, haywards, bread and aletasters and inspectors of meat, fish and leather. These were not of course paid civil servants, but ordinary members of the community elected in turn to see that its bye-laws and the statutes of the realm were observed.

## Living under the Law

The citizen of Newmarket had of course to live under both the statutes of the realm and the bye-laws of the town. The court rolls of the period show what statutes of the realm were deemed to be of importance in Newmarket. There was for example King Henry VIII's statute of 1541 requiring that all his subjects should 'use and exercise shotinge in long bowes, and also have a bowe and arrowes contynuallye readye in his house'.[22] Nothing much seems to have happened about this until 1578 when twenty-six young men were each fined 6s 8d for not having bows and arrows. The same statute of 1541 decreed that every town should have its own archery butts and that the 'inhabitants shall exercise them selfes with longe bowes in shotinge at the same and els where in holye dayes and other tymes convenient'. In 1595, over fifty years later, it was reported without further comment that the town of Newmarket did not have the prescribed butts.

Under the same act of 1541 King Henry VIII condemned the making of money from the letting of any 'common, house, alley or place of bowlinge' for the playing of any games. Thirty years later three Newmarket men were each fined 6s 8d for encouraging people to play at 'painted cards' and at a game 'vulgarly called Tables', that is backgammon. In 1595 John Pickes was fined 40s for allowing an illegal game called Nine Holes to be played in his garden, and five others were fined 6s 8d for playing it. Nine Holes was probably Nine Men's Morris, a game which could be played indoors or out of doors and seems to have combined the skills of draughts with those of noughts and crosses. Shakespeare describes a wet and stormy season thus:

> The folds stand empty in the drowned field,
> And crows are fatted with the murrain flock:
> The nine men's morris is fill'd up with mud.[23]

All this sounds very innocuous to us in our sophisticated 20th century ears, but these attempts to control the way people spent their leisure seem to be characteristic of the period in which Puritan influences were growing stronger. It is noteworthy that this statute on gaming is in the same act as that on archery, implying that young men should be occupied in more worthwhile pursuits than playing games.

Finally in 1570

> most and in maner all Men have forborne and left the using and wearing of cappes, to the great ympoverishing and utter undoynge of all the . . . company and fellowship of Cappers.

It was therefore ordered that all over six years of age, except

> Maidens, Ladyes and Gentlewomen . . . shall use and weare upon the Saboth and Holy Daye, unles in the tyme of travel . . . upon their Head one cappe of Woll Knytt, thicked and dressed in England . . . and only dressed and fynished by some of the Trade or science of Cappers.[24]

Those not so wearing caps were to be fined 3s 4d 'for evry daye not so wearing'. Twenty-five years later the court at Newmarket noted that the inhabitants do not wear caps as prescribed by statute on Sundays and holy days; no one however was actually fined.

Although we have not Newmarket court rolls for the years in which these statutes were passed, we are intrigued by the fact that it was many years after their passing that Newmarket people were expected to observe them. Did it take twenty years or more for a statute passed at Westminster to filter down to a small market town like Newmarket? Or was it that a legalistically minded agent of the lord of the manor, looking through the statute book, discovered ways in which he could increase the manorial income? Or was it that people were deliberately reactivating older legislation to suit a growing Puritan morality?

Offences against the law of the land recorded in the 16th century in Newmarket have in one respect an air of respectability lacking in those of the early 15th. The ten surviving leet rolls for the years 1399–1412 recorded over 130 cases of assault, such as 'John Bocher assaulted Peter Fydeler and drew blood from him with his knife (fined 4d)'. In the eight years between 1565 and 1595 for which similar rolls survive only ten cases of such assault are recorded. What inferences can be drawn from this?

Were social conditions better? Was there less poverty? Had social habits changed?

Bye-laws passed by the local court were of course regarded as of greater importance since they nearly always reflected local problems requiring some immediate action or affecting the well-being of the community as a whole. Dung in the High Street, grazing on Market Means, gleaning, trespassing with cattle and pigs, fencing (to keep cattle out as well as in), curbs and ropes for wells, repair of shops or houses in a dangerous state, encroachment and much else were all subjects of bye-laws during this century. Of interest is that passed in 1576, requiring 'no person able to work any harvest worke to glean before the person [parson?] hath cryed hokey, under penalty of 10d'. The Horkey Suppers held in All Saints' Church at harvest time are perhaps the sole survivors of this bye-law.

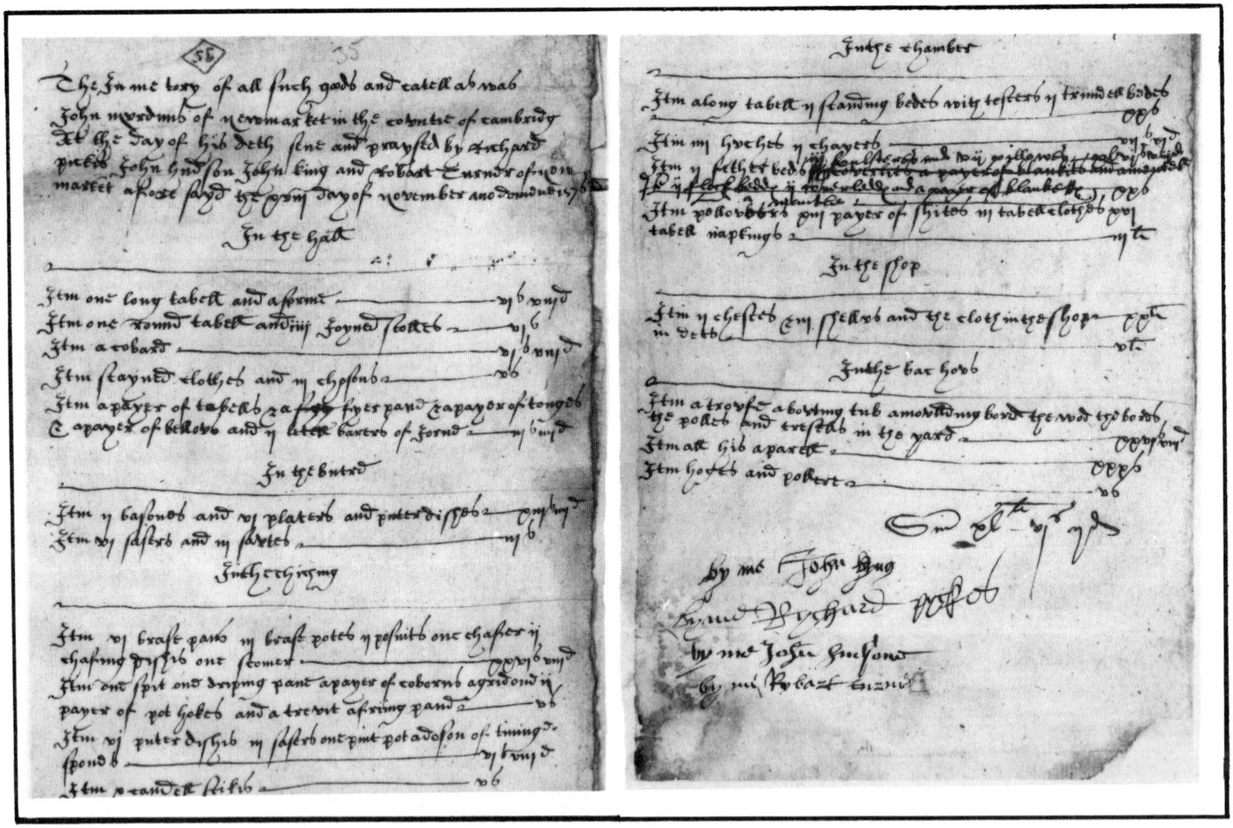
The Inventory of all such goods and catell as was
John Murdun of Newmarket in the countie of Cambridge
at the day of his deth sene and praysed by Richard

In the hall

In the buttre

In the kitchinge

In the chamber

In the shop

In the bar house

**Illustration 16** **The inventory of John Murdun, 1576**

**In order to obtain probate the goods and chattels of the dead man were seen and valued by two or more of his neighbours, who went from room to room, listing and valuing his goods and chattels. Notice the 'chestes', 'shellvs' and the cloth in his shop; he was a draper. For a discussion of the rooms in his house see page 58.**

## The Poor

The poor do not appear as such very often in our contemporary local documents. It may well be that some 30 per cent of those who lived in Newmarket could be described as poor. Certainly we know from the amount of legislation passed at the end of Queen Elizabeth's reign that poverty was then rife throughout England. As we have seen, in 1595 John Hudson was fined, under a local bye-law, 40s for harbouring poor people at the Star; a similar bye-law of 1579 prohibited anyone having sub-tenants in his house, and ordered their expulsion before the coming Michaelmas Day. Later, in 1606, sub-tenants were only permitted with the consent of four freeholders of the town. All this was to ensure that the poor were not attracted into the town and so became chargeable to its residents. We are familiar even today with communities concerned to protect themselves from the problems created by the presence of the poor and underprivileged in their midst.

This does not however mean that individuals were lacking in their generosity to the poor. Testators frequently made such provision in their wills. In the 16th century this seems to have taken three forms. First inherited from the 15th century were the (self-regarding) benefactions of, say, 1d to every poor person attending the funeral, self-regarding in the sense that this ensured that more people would pray for the testator's soul. Secondly there were short-term benefactions in cash or food and drink for the poor, benefactions which did not stipulate attendance at the funeral and were therefore less self-interested. So Richard Trowle, a draper, in 1594 willed that on the day of his funeral ten dozen penny breads, five dozen halfpenny breads and two barrels of beer were to be given to the poor.[25] No doubt they were given out at the church porch, so there was some pressure on the poor to be present at the funeral, but basically self-regard does not seem to have been the dominant motive. Thirdly there were benefactions which were long-term and concerned for the good of the poor and not primarily for the soul of the testator. Thus John Archer in 1550 gave a barrel of red herrings and two loads of faggots yearly in Lent and at Christmas to 'the poore people of the Towneship of Newmarkett', to be bought out of the profits of the Maidenhead (see plan D on pages 32 33). Forty years later Samuel Hudson left 20s yearly for the poor on much the same terms, out of the profits of the Prince's Arms.[26] These and similar long-term benefactions, as often as not from the profits of alehouses, were generally to be distributed at the discretion of the churchwardens. John Archer's and Samuel Hudson's benefactions are still disbursed, in cash at Christmas every year at St Mary's Church by the churchwardens.

**Illustration 17**  A sixteenth century draper's shop

61

## The Reformation

This threefold pattern of giving reflects one effect of the Reformation on Newmarket people. It has been said for example that giving to the poor in the 16th century tended to take the place of giving for the fabric and ornaments of the church, partly due perhaps to an injunction of King Henry VIII in 1536, suggesting that gifts to the poor were more profitable to the soul's health.[27] Newmarket wills certainly confirm this. After 1544 only three wills specifically mention bequests for church fabric and ornaments. Gifts for copes, altar cloths, the roodloft of St Mary's Church, the bells of All Saints' Church, the glazing of a window in St Mary's and the maintenance of church fabric all appear in wills made before 1544. Of the three wills after 1544 which mention gifts to the church, those of John Kyrbie in 1577 and of Roger Borowdale in 1602, included gifts of cash for the repair of St Mary's Church tower.[28]

The third will of those after 1544 which mention gifts to the church, that of Thomas Borowdale in 1559, is perhaps the most interesting, for several reasons.[29] First he combined gifts to the church with long-term benefactions to the poor. His gifts to All Saints' Church included 'my Clocke which now standyth framed in the saide Churche', two church service books (an antiphoner and a processioner), altar cloths of 'blew Satten with Flowers of gold' and a white vestment. As for the poor they were to be given 2 marks (26s 8d) yearly out of the sale of his houses. Secondly he made his will in 1559, the second year of Queen Elizabeth's reign. He had seen King Henry VIII throw off the authority of the Papacy, he had seen King Edward VI push the Protestant cause further still and he had seen Queen Mary reverse the process. We can hardly wonder that in his will his gifts to All Saints' Church contain the proviso 'always that if the service of God be withdrawne and not maynteyned so that the seid bookes, vestements and other my legaces before given to the same church shall not serve for thintentes aforeseid', his executors could dispose of them elsewhere. That sentence perhaps expresses the hope that there would be no more changes.

Thomas Borowdale was a parishioner of All Saints' Church in 1553 when an inventory of the churchplate, vestments and bells was made. This was the sixth year of King Edward VI's reign and orders had been given that images, statues, vestments, ornaments and service books should be thrown out of the churches. Of all the many gifts that had been made to the church over the years, there was very little left when the commissioners came to inspect it, only a chalice, two copes, two vestments and three bells in the steeple. They ordered that the chalice, one cope and one vestment should be kept 'for thonlie mayntenance of dyvyne servyce in the saide parishe churche'.[30] We suspect that Thomas Borowdale, a prudent parishioner, had seen to it that the two service books, the blue satin altar cloths and the white vestment were not visible for inspection when the commissioners arrived, and that when he died in 1559 he was in fact giving back to All Saints' Church what had originally belonged to it!

There is one other small indication of the effect of the Reformation on people in Newmarket. In pre-Reformation days all testators commended their souls to God in such formal terms as: 'I commend my soul to God Almighty, the blessed Virgin Mary and the holy company of heaven.' When Walter Button made his will in 1588 the commendation of his soul deserves printing in full, as an example of evangelical piety at its most fulsome:

> I most reverently commend my soule into the hands of Almyghtye God, in whome is all my hope & assurance protestinge here before heaven & earthe that I am fullie assured & livelye perswaded by the Spiritt of God that I was before all worldes elected to be Fellowe heyre with Jesus Christe in whose merritts or worthinesse my synnes are covered in the treasures of eternal happiness, and nowe after the effectual callinge of his worde, that I am saved, onely and frelye by the meare mercy of God through Faythe apprehendinge or layinge hould uppon his sonne Jesus Christ, without any respect of myne owne merritts or deservinges, beinge of them selves more filthye than a foule ragge wrapped up in corrupte blode as sayeth the prophet.[31]

More suited perhaps to our taste is the commendation of Thomas Turner in which he combines both Catholic tradition and Protestant piety in the words:

> I commend my soul to Christ Jesus, trusting by the merits of his passion to have after this mortal life fruition of his presence wherefor I desire the Blessed Virgin Mary his mother with all the holy company to pray for me and with me.[32]

## Women and Children

A picture of Newmarket in the 16th century would not be complete without mention of children and women. Children appear frequently in wills of course as recipients of legacies, generally to be received when they reach a mature age, or, in the case of girls, on their wedding day. There is a rather touching concern on the part of some young husbands on their deathbeds for 'the child that is now in my wife's belly'. Middle class folk sometimes expressed concern for the education of their children. Henry Funston for example in 1536 left certain lands to his wife Margaret in order that she might 'find' their son Christopher 'at school until he be 21'.[33] Walter Button's legacy of certain shops to his wife Agnes in 1588 was made with the wish that she should bring up their son Walter 'in literature' until he was twenty years old.[34] We know nothing about education in Newmarket at this time, but no doubt there were a few children going round with their hornbooks as in the illustration opposite.

The death of husbands with young families very often under the age of twenty-one meant a surfeit of widows. Many of them married again (as indeed of course did many widowers), had another family by their second husband and then survived him. Some were clearly very poor and had to earn their own living, like Elizabeth Coward, who was a baker and left a flockbed, a bolster and a pair of sheets to her daughter-in-law, and the residue of her property (for what it was worth) to her three daughters.[35] Others were comparatively well off, generally giving very precise instructions in their wills as to how their goods and chattels were to be allocated by

their executors. Joan Fookes, for example, who survived two husbands, must have gone through her house room by room before she made her will, allocating every single item (over eighty in all) to her daughters, granddaughters and friends.[36] She was evidently a very competent woman. No doubt there were many others like her, if we may judge from the fact that many a 16th century husband in Newmarket made his wife the sole executrix of his will.

Illustration 18

A sixteenth century schoolboy reading his hornbook

This consisted of a piece of paper or parchment set in a wooden or bone tablet, covered with transparent horn (the 16th century equivalent of plastic). The rod in his hand was to hang it from his belt when not in use, and possibly to circle the letters he was reading. (The book from which this illustration was taken was the first book specially printed for children, in 1578.)

We have reached the end of the first stage of Newmarket's history. The picture that has emerged has been that of a small market town, dominated by its middle class, with its complement of innkeepers, retailers and craftsmen, contributing by their skills to the life of the community, the neighbouring villages and travellers on their way through it between London and Norwich. No one living in Newmarket in 1600 could possibly have imagined that this inconspicuous and insignificant place would become in twenty-five years the site of a royal palace and in the 20th century the centre of horse racing and breeding in England, if not in the world.

# THE ARCHAEOLOGY OF NEWMARKET

*Ivan E. Moore*

Disregarding the immediate parish boundaries, not existing in antiquity, Newmarket was not devoid of inhabitants, temporary or permanent, during the millenium before written records became available. This was largely the result of geographical factors and the accompanying soil conditions.

Newmarket could be reached from the north by means of the Fenland river system and from both north and south along a chalk belt running from north west Norfolk to the south west around Salisbury Plain; a route to become known as the Icknield Way with its local parallel Street Way. This belt narrows and the route becomes more restricted as it approaches Newmarket to pass between the heavy clayland, afforested in ancient time, of central Suffolk to the east and the swampy Fenland to the west. Here expanses of well drained land with slow moving streams to provide a water supply encouraged short or prolonged settlement of immigrants to the region. In instances the same areas attracted occupation throughout all periods.

Though it may be presumed there was a Neolithic presence in view of other works of the period at not too great a distance, such as the cursus at Fornham All Saints and the settlement at Hurst Fen, Mildenhall, only an axe and some arrowheads of that age have been reported. The first of the earlier peoples to leave their mark were the Beaker folk. Two burials of the period are known in Newmarket itself, actually in the parish of Exning, and there are others in adjoining parishes. One of these burials in Edinburgh Road comprised two graves, one containing a male adult, five children and a baby, and the one

adjoining a female adult. The other burial in Fordham Road, after an anatomical examination of the remains, was shown to be that of a female who had suffered extreme injuries in her life-time. Small drinking vessels normally accompanied such burial where the body was interred in the foetal position. Though only sherds were noted at Edinburgh and Fordham Roads undamaged vessels have been recovered from similar burials to the north of the town, while an ogival dagger and axe-hammer from that at Chippenham indicate a link with the Wessex culture of Salisbury Plain, and suggest some movement of peoples.

Cinerary urns belonging to the Middle Bronze Age, when cremation of the dead was practised, were recovered when barrows were destroyed on the Heath in the 19th century in the preparation of courses for horse racing. Two more such barrows are known north of the town.

Little metal work belonging to the Bronze Age is recorded for Newmarket itself, except in error in the instance of a hoard from Exning, but the founder's hoard from Isleham and a sword and fragments of others together with some metal from Chippenham bear witness to smiths in the area in the Late Bronze Age.

Apart from scattered sherds and a coin of Addedomarus *c.*20 B.C., little has come to light belonging to the Iron Age but the warrior burial at Snailwell, furnished with spindle-shaped amphorae and containing also Gallo-Belgic pottery, datable to the mid 1st century, shows there was some movement from the south into the region around the time of the Roman invasion. A scatter of items in a nearby parish included Late Iron Age and Roman material.

The Roman period itself is represented by a scattered open settlement, so characteristic of Suffolk, in the Hamilton Stud area. On this site wells have been detected, one of which was excavated, and from it have come finds of pottery and cremation burials. At Landwade an aisled building has been excavated. The occupation here had its beginnings in the late 1st century and the building itself was rebuilt and enlarged to the extent of having added to it a paved hypocausted room at one end and a bath house at the other by the time it was destroyed by fire in the early fourth century. There was another dwelling at not too great a distance at Fordham and close by in Snailwell there is a record of a late 2nd century cremation burial. Though there is no evidence on the ground it has been supposed that some trackway, serving as a road in Roman times, crossed the area to link up at Cambridge with the road proceeding northward from Haverhill, 'Wool Street'.

What happened at the close of the Roman period and in the Anglo Saxon period is shrouded in mystery. The Devil's Dyke, built across the chalk belt and barring the way, the most outstanding antiquity of Newmarket and the best preserved of a series of dykes in Cambridgeshire. It is now known that it was constructed sometime after A.D. 350 and the techniques employed in its building understood. It was apparently abandoned at about A.D. 1000. Only a series of options are available as to its initial function. The pagan Saxon presence is represented by a cemetery at Windmill Hill, Exning, where an extended skeleton with a spear and shield boss was recovered in 1981, and the Middle or Late Saxon period by a dwelling found when excavating a moat in 1973. It is at this point in time that the document begins to take over from features and artefacts.

## SOURCES

Records of the Archaeological Units of Suffolk and Cambridgeshire; British Museum; Moyes Hall Museum, Bury St Edmunds; *Journal of Roman Studies* XLIX, 123 and L, 228.

## BIBLIOGRAPHY

Dewhurst, P.C., 'Wool Street, Cambridgeshire', *Proceedings of the Cambridge Antiquarian Society,* LVI–LVII (1963), 42–60

Fox, C., *The Archaeology of the Cambridgeshire Region,* Cambridge (1923)

Johnson, D.E. and Hartley, B.R., 'A Roman Well at Exning', *Proc. Cambridge Antiq. Soc.,* LII (1959), 11–20

Leaf, C.S., 'Two Bronze Age Barrows at Chippenham, Cambridgeshire', *Proc. Cambridge Antiq. Soc.,* XXXVI (1936), 134–155

Leaf, C.S., 'Further Excavations in Bronze Age Barrows at Chippenham, Cambridgeshire', *Proc. Cambridge Antiq. Soc.,* XXXIX (1940), 29–68

Lethbridge, T.C., 'Excavation of the Snailwell Group of Bronze Age Barrows', *Proc. Cambridge Antiq. Soc.,* XLIII (1950), 30–49

Lethbridge, T.C., 'Burial of an Iron Age Warrior at Snailwell', *Proc. Cambridge Antiq. Soc.,* XLVII (1954), 25–37

Martin, E.A., 'The Excavation of a Moat at Exning', *East Anglian Archaeology,* I (1975), 24–38

Martin, E.A., 'The Excavation of Two Tumuli on Waterfall Farm, Chippenham', *Proc. Cambridge Antiq. Soc.,* LXVI (1977), 1–21

Moore, I.E., 'Roman Suffolk', *Proceedings of the Suffolk Institute of Archaeology,* XXIV (1948), 163–181

Prigg, H., 'On the Recent Discovery of a Bronze Sword, at Chippenham, Cambridgeshire', *Proc. Suffolk Inst. Archaeol.,* VI (1888), 183–194. (In Fitzwilliam Museum, Cambridge)

Sturge, W. Allen, 'Early Man', *Victoria County History, Suffolk,* I (1911)

Taylor, B.H. and Hill, D., 'The Devil's Dyke Investigations, 1973', *Proc. Cambridge Antiq. Soc.,* LXVI (1977), 123–126

# References

## Chapter One – Pages 1–6
### THE BEGINNINGS
1. Public Record Office, CP 25 (1) 23/9/2
2. P.R.O. E 179/239/242
3. P.R.O. C/60/18, confirmed in C 53/18/26
4. *Hundred Rolls,* Vol. I, p. 49
5. *Hundred Rolls,* Vol. II, p. 199
6. *The East Anglian,* New Series, Vol. XI, p. 79f
7. *Suffolk Green Books,* Vol. IX, p. 102f
8. *Inquisitio Nonarum,* p. 214
9. *Inquisitio Nonarum,* p. 83f
10. *Suffolk Green Books,* Vol. X, p. 229f
11. P.R.O. C 53/48/m4
12. Iveagh (Suffolk), 100, Phillips 3817, Part II, ff. 23–25
13. Domesday Book, Vol. I, f. 189b
14. *Florence of Worcester's Chronicle* (ed. Forster), pp. 177ff
15. Pigot's *Cambridge Directory* (1830), p. 117
16. *British Magazine,* November 1832, p. 230
17. *The Suffolk Review,* I.4, p. 82
18. M. W. Beresford, *New Towns of the Middle Ages,* p. 490
19. W. G. Hoskins, *Fieldwork in Local History,* p. 90
20. Holland's revised translation (1610) of Camden's *Britannia,* p. 459; the entry is not in the first (latin) edition of 1586.
21. *The Cartae Antiquae* (Pipe Roll Society, N.S. Vol. XXXIII), pp. 90f
22. *Liber Rubeus de Scaccario* (ed. H. Hall), Vol. II, p. 478
23. Norman Scarfe, *The Suffolk Landscape,* p. 166
24. Suffolk Record Office (Bury St Edmunds), Acc. 359/3

## Chapter Two – Pages 7–15
### THE CHARACTER OF THE NEW TOWN
1. E. Miller and J. Thatcher, *Medieval England, Rural Society and Economic Change, 1086–1348,* p. 77
2. For details of the Exning manors see W. A. Copinger, *The Manors of Suffolk,* Vol. IV, pp. 156ff
3. For the Well Hall Survey see P.R.O. C 133/50 and for the Newmarket survey see P.R.O. C 133/33/16.
4. For details of the Cambridgeshire manor of Melbourn see *Proceedings of the Cambridgeshire Antiquarian Society,* Vol. XXVIII, pp. 16ff
5. P.R.O. SC 6/766/15

6. See the 15th century account rolls of the manor of Newmarket in the Suffolk Record Office (Bury St Edmunds), Acc. 1476/12.
7. S.R.O. (B), E 3/33/1
8. S.R.O. (B), Acc. 1476/12
9. D. M. Owen, *Church and State in Medieval Lincolnshire,* p. 19
10. S.R.O. (B), 806/1/115
11. S.R.O. (B), Acc. 359/8 and E 3/33/1
12. Tanner's Index, Reg. 31, p. 1284, in the Norfolk Record Office, Norwich
13. Iveagh (Suffolk), 100 Phillips 3817, Part II, ff. 23–25
14. P.R.O. C 53/79
15. *Archaeologia,* Vol. I (1762), pp. 210ff

## Chapter Three – Pages 17–24
### THE WIDER WORLD
1. For full details of the Argentein and Alington families and their connections with Newmarket see J. P. Hore, *The History of Newmarket,* Vol. I, pp. 41–52
2. P.R.O. C. 60/30/8, 10 and 11
3. P.R.O. C 60/79/4
4. P.R.O. C 145/37/26
5. J. P. Hore, *The History of Newmarket,* Vol. I, p. 46
6. Matthew Paris, *Historia Magna* (ed. H. R. Luard), Vol. IV, p. 587
7. According to the article on the Argentein manor of Melbourn in *Proceedings of the Cambridge Antiquarian Society,* Vol. XXVIII, p. 27
8. Matthew Paris, *Historia Magna,* Vol. III, p. 405
9. *Proceedings of the Cambridge Antiquarian Society,* Vol. XXVIII, pp. 16ff
10. *Proceedings of the Cambridge Antiquarian Society,* Vol. LII, pp. 30ff
11. J. P. Hore, *The History of Newmarket,* Vol. I, p. 50
12. Rymer's *Foedera,* Tom. II, Part 1, p. 25
13. D. M. Stenton, *The Pelican History of England,* Vol. III, pp. 81ff
14. Much of the material in this section is taken from P. Ziegler, *The Black Death.* A very readable account of the Black Death in East Anglia may be found in A. Jessopp, *The Coming of the Friars,* pp. 166ff
15. Details of the institutions in the Diocese of Norwich are to be found in the Bishop of Norwich's Registers, in the County Record Office at Norwich, on microfilm at the Suffolk Record Office at Ipswich; those in the Diocese of Ely are to be found in the Bishop of Ely's Registers in the University Library, Cambridge.
16. P. Ziegler, *The Black Death,* p. 177
17. *Victoria County History, Cambridgeshire,* Vol. II, p. 158

**Chapter Three** *(continued)*

18. Diocesan percentages from C. G. Coulton, *The Medieval Panorama*, p. 496
19. Deanery percentages from J. W. F. Shrewsbury, *The History of the Bubonic Plague in the British Isles,* p. 98. In his map of the Diocese of Norwich, Shrewsbury misplaces the Deanery of Fordham, and records as 'unidentified' nine deaneries in Suffolk, some of which, for example Thingoe, are still deaneries today, 600 years later.
20. P.R.O. SC2 156/56/20
21. Henry Knighton, *Chronica* (ed. J. R. Lumby), Vol. II, pp. 58–65, quoted in R. B. Dobson, *The Peasants' Revolt, 1381,* pp. 60f
22. Details may be found in R. B. Dobson, *The Peasants' Revolt, 1381,* pp. 63ff
23. P.R.O. C 60/249/20
24. P.R.O. C 60/288/4
25. According to *The East Anglian,* O.S. Vol. IV, p. 137, from which this reference is taken, William Cratfield was Rector of Wrotham in Norfolk. Diocesan institution lists show no rector of that name at Wrotham, but that a William de Cratfield was Rector of Wortham Eastgate in Suffolk from 1401 to 1408 (see *East Anglian Miscellany,* 1920, Item no. 5778); I am indebted to Mr Peter Northeast for this correction.
26. Thomas Nashe, *Pierce Penniless,* in Selected Writings (ed. S. Wells), p. 29
27. *State Papers, Charles I, 1649–50,* p. 81
28. P.R.O. C 66/314/9d
29. Much of the material in this section is taken from R. B. Dobson, *The Peasants' Revolt, 1381* and E. Powell, *The Rising in East Anglia in 1381.*
30. *The East Anglian,* N.S. Vol. VI, pp. 81ff and 137f
31. *The East Anglian,* N.S. Vol. VI, pp. 97f
32. The first reference to St Tebold is to be found in John Farlee's will of 1434 (Norfolk Record Office, Norwich, Probate 146 Surflete).
33. R. B. Dobson, *The Peasants' Revolt, 1381,* pp. 172 ff

**Chapter Four – Pages 25–30**
**THE ECONOMY OF THE NEW TOWN**

1. British Library, Add. Charter 25867 (Newmarket) and P.R.O. SC 6/766/16 (Ditton Valens)
2. S.R.O. (B), E 18/455/3. It is interesting to note that at Mildenhall in 1411 villeins were able to commute their 'boon works' for cash.
3. P.R.O. SC 6/766/15
4. S.R.O. (B), Acc. 359/3
5. S.R.O. (B), Acc. 359/3
6. See the plan of Laxton, published by Pictorial Charts Education Trust, 27 Kirchen Street, London W13 0UD.

7. Account Rolls for 1428–1440 S.R.O. (B), Acc. 1476/12, for 1472/3 Acc. 359/3 and for 1473–1483 Acc. 1476/13
8. John Burnett in *A History of the Cost of Living* (Pelican 1969) suggests a multiplier of forty for a composite list of consumables for the years 1351–1475 and 1954.

**Chapter Five – Pages 31–42**
**THE FIFTEENTH CENTURY: THE HIGH STREET**

1. The local documents referred to throughout this chapter are:
   (i) the wills of twenty 15th century Newmarket men and women; these are mostly preserved in the Suffolk Record Office in Bury St Edmunds. I have transcribed and translated them in my *Twenty Newmarket Wills 1439–1497;*
   (ii) the court rolls for the manor of Newmarket for 1399–1413, preserved in the Suffolk Record Office at Bury St Edmunds, Ref. Acc. 1476/1–48.
2. S.R.O. (B), Acc. 359/3
3. P.R.O. C 135/49 no. 21/2
4. S.R.O. (B), 806/1/115
5. P.R.O. DL 28/5/8
6. *Vide* A. Luders, *Statutes of the Realm,* Volume I, pp. 199f
7. S.R.O. (B), E 18/451/1
8. S.R.O. (B), E 3/33/1
9. S.R.O. (B), Acc. 359/8
10. C. M. Hood, 'An East Anglian Contemporary of Pepys', *Norfolk Archaeology,* XXII, p. 152

**Chapter Six – Pages 43–50**
**THE FIFTEENTH CENTURY: THE MARKET**

1. See my article in *The Suffolk Review*, Vol. 4, No. 4, pp. 191ff
2. John Stow, *Survey of London* (Oxford 1971), Vol. I, p.346
3. S.R.O. (B), Acc. 1476/1/32
4. S.R.O. (B), Acc. 359/3
5. I have conflated the wording of two statutes relating to Weights and Measures in 1351 and 1353, printed in A. Luders, *Statutes of the Realm,* Vol. I, pp. 321 and 337.
6. S.R.O. (B), Acc. 1476/1/19
7. S.R.O. (B), Acc. 1476/1/14
8. S.R.O. (B), Acc. 1476/1/45
9. *The Index of Court Rolls* was published in 1896. Those who compiled it were classical scholars and translated 'Curia Nundinarum' as market court in accordance with classical usage. Medieval writers used the phrase for a fair court and 'Curia Mercati' or 'Curia Fori' to describe a market court.

**Chapter Six** *(continued)*

10. S.R.O. (B), Acc. 1476/1/1−48 contains the rolls for all the four Newmarket courts for the years 1399−1412. The market court rolls are in membranes 1, 5, 6, 7, 11, 13, 15, 17, 19, 20, 21, 25, 28, 29, 33, 35, 36, 40, 41, 43, 46, 47. A copy of my transcription of these rolls is in the Suffolk Record Office at Bury St Edmunds. I have examined the market court at Newmarket in more detail in an article in the *Proceedings of the Suffolk Institute of Archaeology and History* for 1981.
11. The court rolls for the court at Barton Gate, Ely may be seen at the University Library, Cambridge, E 1/1/1−3, and those for Sudbury at the Public Record Office, Chancery Lane, SC2 203/1ff.
12. Simon Funston's will may be seen in the Suffolk Record Office, Bury St Edmunds, Probate Boner 92. The reference to Henry Funston may be found in the British Library, Add. MS. 5823, f. 239.

**Chapter Seven — Pages 51−64**
**THE SIXTEENTH CENTURY**

1. The local documents which I have consulted in this chapter have been the court rolls of the manor in the Suffolk Record Office at Bury St Edmunds, Acc. 359/4−8 and 1476/2−4, and all the wills in that office, the Norfolk Record Office and the Public Record Office (Prerogative Court of Canterbury). I am most grateful to Peter Northeast for allowing me to use his abstracts of many of these wills.
2. Norfolk Record Office (Norwich), Dep. 1449−1512, I
3. P.R.O. (P.C.C.), 27 Porch
4. S.R.O. (B), E 3/33/1
5. P.R.O. (P.C.C.) 47 Mellershe
6. S.R.O. (B), Prob. Coole 541
7. S.R.O. (B), Prob. Bacon 564
8. S.R.O. (B), Prob. Whiting 464
9. S.R.O. (B), Prob. Colman 40
10. William Bullein, *A Booke of Simples* (1562), fol. xlvi
11. *The Essex Review*, Vol. XIX, pp. 57−64; I owe this reference to Peter Northeast
12. S.R.O. (B), IC 1500/3/1/29
13. P.R.O. E 182/345
14. P.R.O. E 182/377. In the court rolls for the Newmarket manor for the years 1577−1583 thirty people were fined on an average each year as *cupidinarii* for making excessive profits; it should mean extortioners; I have taken it to apply to retailers in general.
15. P.R.O. (P.C.C.), 35 Montague
16. A. Luders, *Statutes of the Realm*, Vol. IV, Pt. i, pp. 168ff
17. *Patent Rolls (1554−5)*, p. 127
18. *State Papers (1603−10)*, p. 449
19. A. Luders, *Statutes of the Realm*, Vol. I, p. 308
20. S.R.O. (B), Prob. Everston 251
21. S.R.O. (B), IC 1500/3/1/35
22. A. Luders, *Statutes of the Realm*, Vol.III, pp. 838f
23. *A Midsummer Night's Dream*, Act II, Scene ii
24. A Luders, *Statutes of the Realm*, Vol. IV, Pt. i, p. 555
25. P.R.O. (P.C.C.), 5 Scott
26. S.R.O. (B), Prob. Coole 494 and Bacon 133
27. I owe this reference to Peter Northeast.
28. P.R.O. (P.C.C.), 16 Langley and S.R.O. (B), Prob. Whiting 468
29. Norfolk Record Office (Norwich), Prob. Woodcocke 322
30. *The East Anglian*, N.S. Vol. VIII, p. 229
31. S.R.O. (B), Prob. Bacon 564
32. S.R.O. (B), Prob. Coole 488
33. P.R.O. (P.C.C.), 4 Crumwell
34. S.R.O. (B), Prob. Bacon 564
35. S.R.O. (B), Prob. Browne 388
36. S.R.O. (B), Prob. Bloomfield 219

# Index